Issues in Setting Standards

Issues in Setting Standards:
Establishing Comparabilities

Edited by

Bill Boyle and Tom Christie

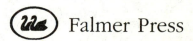 Falmer Press

(A member of the Taylor & Francis Group)
London • Washington, D.C.

UK   The Falmer Press, 4 John Street, London WC1N 2ET
USA   The Falmer Press, Taylor & Francis Inc., 1900 Frost Road, Suite 101,
      Bristol, PA 19007

First published in 1996

**A catalogue record for this book is available from the British
Library**

**Library of Congress Cataloging-in-Publication Data are
available on request**

ISBN 0 7507 0481 0 cased
ISBN 0 7507 0482 9 paper

Jacket design by Caroline Archer

Typeset in 10/12 pt Garamond by
Graphicraft Typesetters Ltd., Hong Kong.

*Printed in Great Britain by Burgess Science Press, Basingstoke on
paper which has a specified pH value on final paper manufacture
of not less than 7.5 and is therefore 'acid free'.*

Contents

Contents

Test Issues

List of Figures and Tables

Figures

Tables

Introduction

The setting of educational standards of achievement, the routes by which those standards are obtained and their relative comparabilities are research issues of national and international concern. The notion of an international educational standard and the gathering of evidence that would be required to substantiate this is an intriguing one. At present any evidence, if so it can be called, is derived from surveys by the International Association for the Evaluation of Educational Achievement such as the first and second international mathematics and science studies (FIMS and SIMS). A Third International Mathematics and Science Study (TIMSS) is currently ongoing.

It was to address the issue of international standards that, in September 1994, Professor Tom Christie, Director of the Centre for Formative Assessment Studies (CFAS), based at the School of Education at the University of Manchester, hosted the 'Setting Standards: Establishing Comparabilities' conference. Attended by many respected figures from the British and European assessment 'industry', the conference was associated with the European Association for Research in Learning and Instruction (EARLI). EARLI's main aim is to promote empirical and theoretical research into processes of learning, development and instruction in educational or training settings, with a Special Interest Group (SIG 13) dedicated to Assessment and Evaluation issues.

From the contributors to the conference a selection of papers has been collected for this book. They have been arranged for ease of access within categories, i.e. international, national and test specific issues. However, across these categories a common theme emerges for discussion, namely the movement in many countries to establish outcomes-oriented standards for education, an almost global preoccupation with quality control models concerned solely with outcomes at the expense of processes. The papers clearly represent a broad church, crossing national and international boundaries. Professor Wynne Harlen (Director, Scottish Council for Research in Education) has been involved in National Curriculum developments since the initial Key Stage One consortia were contracted by SEAC in 1988 and laments that teachers' assessments are being further devalued because they are seen as providing 'soft' data compared to 'hard' test outcomes. Dylan Wiliam unveils the conflict between policy and data oriented methods of test construction and illustrates how the test constructor's cut-score or level threshold can be absolute in producing impressions of rising or falling standards, the political imperative or chance variation?

Professor Roger Murphy indicates that comparability of standards in higher education in Britain is grossly under-researched. Facts that have been unearthed, such as that students entering some universities in 1991–92 were five times as likely to achieve a first class honours degree than those entering certain other universities, and that Cambridge University awarded first class honours degrees to 24 per cent of its graduates in 1993–94 (more than 10 per cent higher than any other university) are sufficiently worrying to warrant pursuing. However, Murphy does conclude that as subject comparability within-university cannot be guaranteed, cross-university equivalence in ninety-two institutions is a pointless stretching of public confidence.

International standard setting dimensions are provided by a view from within the International Baccalaureate Organization by its Director, Ian Walker, and by comparisons across ten of the twenty-five Organization for Economic Co-operation and Development (OECD) countries by Dr John Townshend's account of the background to the compilation of the Performance Standards in Education report.

Kari Smith's thesis that learner-centred teaching requires learner-centred assessment is based on and illustrated from the experiences of her work at Haifa University, Israel, while her chapter's title 'Humanistic education requires humanistic assessment' provides a suitably optimistic atmosphere to invite you to read on.

Bill Boyle

International Issues

1 Comparing Performance Standards in Education

John Townshend

Summary

The project which is described here is a joint Organization for Economic Cooperation and Development (OECD)/United States Government initiative, entitled Performance Standards in Education. It involves ten of the twenty-five OECD countries the United States (US), United Kingdom (UK), France, Spain, Germany, Sweden, Australia, Japan, Canada/Ontario, and Ireland, chosen so as to be broadly representative. Four of them are federal and six are unitary states. Their education systems are correspondingly diverse, ranging from highly centralized to relatively decentralized. Reports have been written by experts in these countries and these have been used to produce a synthesis report. Early in October 1994 a seminar was held in Paris, at which seventeen OECD members were represented, to discuss the findings and issues emerging from the first phase of the project. This chapter sets out the context within which the project was established, presents the methods used in the case studies, and discusses some of the important issues which are emerging. The reports will be collated together with contextual and analytical material in an OECD publication in 1995 provisionally entitled 'Students Performance Standards'.

Introduction

The context in which the project was launched is the move in many OECD countries to establish outcomes-oriented standards for education. The UK has been in the vanguard of this movement. The move from concern for educational processes to a preoccupation with outcomes seems to stem from a fairly widespread dissatisfaction with the performance of students, or perhaps it would be more accurate to say with the perceived mismatch between educational outcomes and society's needs. From the contextual sections of the ten country reports it is evident that those OECD countries participating in the project share these concerns, to varying degrees. The studies show that performance standards cannot be considered in isolation from such factors as the recent expansion of participation rates in upper secondary education or major changes in school organization and pedagogical methods. In most countries the pressure for higher standards is accompanied by budgetary constraints on educational expenditure.

Reforms are under way or being planned in most of them. The concerns seem to relate to several factors, including the awareness of the demands placed on educational systems by global economic competition, especially in the new technologies, and the movement towards more accountability in government and public life. There is little hard evidence of a fall in standards but a widespread belief that, at the least, standards are failing to keep pace with employment-related requirements, especially in the most technologically advanced sectors. A related problem is the existence in most countries of an educational underclass, unemployable in jobs where a minimum of skills and knowledge is required. The accountability movement has led governments and others to focus attention more selectively on those aspects and institutions in education systems which do not appear to be performing adequately. To do this effectively some indicators of performance are required. The degree of concern varies. In some countries, such as Germany and Japan, it is relatively low and is focused on only a few specific aspects of the educational system.

Goals 2000

Dissatisfaction is most acute in the English-speaking countries, particularly the UK and the US. In the UK it led in 1988 to legislation creating a National Curriculum and national assessment procedures. In the US it has led to the bipartisan education reform which was enacted earlier this year and which is known as Goals 2000. Goals 2000 is an important milestone in the debate about standards in the US which has grown ever fiercer since the publication in 1983 of the report by the National Commission on Excellence in Education called rather provocatively 'A Nation at Risk'. It is difficult to exaggerate the impact of this report. A quotation gives the flavour:

> If an unfriendly power had attempted to impose on America the mediocre educational performance that exists today, we might well have viewed it as an act of war. As it stands, we have allowed this to happen to ourselves...

Some of the hyperbole can be put down to the need to dramatize issues in order to allow the federal government some purchase over educational matters which are, constitutionally, largely in the domain of the States. Nevertheless, the debate over standards in the US is intense and widespread.

Goals 2000 sets a challenging agenda for American education. Two of the six goals exemplify this challenge:

> By the year 2000, American students will leave grades four, eight and twelve having demonstrated competency in challenging subject matter

including English, mathematics, science, history and geography; and every school in America will ensure that all students learn to use their minds well, so that they may be prepared for responsible citizenship, further learning, and productive employment in our modern economy. (Goal 3)

By the year 2000, US students will be first in the world in science and mathematics achievement. (Goal 4)

Implicit in that last goal is the notion of an international educational standard and in fact the debate in the US has been structured partly around international comparisons. From the shock of the launch of Sputnik by the Soviet Union in the late 1950s, the US has been haunted by the notion that its industrial and, until the end of the Cold War, military rivals were ahead in scientific know-how. The Soviet Union has now been replaced by Japan and Germany as the point of reference, but the theme is the same. The argument is that poor educational standards, particularly in science and mathematics, are undermining US performance in high technology industries. The evidence, such as it is, comes very largely from the surveys by the International Association for the Evaluation of Educational Achievement (IEA). The best known of these are probably the first and second international mathematics and science studies (FIMS and SIMS). A Third International Mathematics and Science Study (TIMSS) is currently underway. From the inception of the IEA in the early 1960s the US has been its major backer.

IEA studies have consistently shown US students to be underperforming in mathematics and science compared with Japanese and some European students. How much reliance should be placed on such evidence is a question which is much debated in research circles in America and elsewhere. The general consensus appears to be that however suspect some aspects of the IEA studies may be, the broad picture of American student achievement is fair. IEA studies have been useful in pointing to some of the reasons for this under-performance. IEA curriculum analysis has demonstrated, for example, that American curriculum coverage in these subjects is fragmented and less challenging in content than the curriculum in Japan, France or Germany. Hence the concern of Goals 2000 to make American curriculum more challenging.

Federal action to promote, for example, a National Curriculum is ruled out by the constitution. What Goals 2000 promotes is a voluntary association of school districts, States and the federal authorities to define guidelines for more challenging syllabuses in the eight subject areas which are set out as the essential core curriculum. This initiative builds on work done with volunteer States and school districts over several years by the New Standards Project. Currently, too, federal support is being provided for subject committees to produce model 'national' syllabuses. Those for geography and arts have already been published. In return for substantial federal funding, States will undertake to implement the new content and monitor performance standards.

Some educational experts and politicians are worried about the effect on equity and educational opportunity of standard-setting. Given the litigious nature of American society there is concern that before students are tested against new and demanding criteria, they should have had clearly visible comprehensive opportunities to learn the subject matter being tested.

Performance Standards

The OECD has undertaken its project on Performance Standards with the aims of achieving descriptive outlines of the standard-setting procedures in a range of OECD countries and of teasing out common issues and solutions. The choice of experts was a crucial step since the requirement was for a good knowledge of the national system together with an awareness of the international context and relevant research. A semi-structured questionnaire was drawn up to guide the authors and to provide the basis of a common structure for the case-study reports. The guidelines are organized in seven sections, each of which includes a number of detailed questions:

1 reasons for concern about standards;
2 differences in achievement;
3 setting standards;
4 procedures and methods;
5 preconditions and problems;
6 policy formulation and decision-making;
7 the international dimension.

Not all of these sections are of equal weight or importance. Sections (iii) setting standards and (iv) procedures and methods are the most important and substantial. They focus on how countries define, determine and monitor standards.

When OECD received the first drafts of the country case-study reports from the experts it became clear that, given the diversity of the situations they were describing, it would be a mistake to confine them within a straitjacket. Too rigid a format risked losing some of the feel for differing priorities and emphases which was the point of the research. The experts' brief therefore made it clear that, provided the basic information required was included, they could organize the material and regroup the sections as best fitted their system. They were also encouraged to focus on aspects of their systems which could be of particular interest to other countries. For example the Irish government went to great lengths to organize a national debate to attempt to create a consensus around basic concepts for reform. The Irish expert was asked to describe this process and to assess the outcomes. Other experts focused on aspects of the standard-setting process, for example the German expert described what he referred to as a 'self-stabilizing system' which gives great responsibility to teachers in monitoring and setting standards. The result is a set of reports which cover common ground but which also give a very strong sense of the diversity of problems, perspectives and approaches to reform within these national systems.

The reports provide substantial evidence of how standards are set in these countries. In most of them standards still refer mainly to the performance of students who take terminal secondary examinations at 18+. It is only since the 1980s that most countries have set out to produce baseline data for monitoring the educational achievement of all pupils throughout compulsory schooling. Four approaches are used, though few countries use all of them:

1   national diagnostic tests;
2   large-scale national surveys;
3   standardized testing;
4   international surveys.

Again it is Germany and Japan which have been least affected by these recent developments. In Japan, national testing was tried in the 1950s and 1960s but abandoned because it led to severe competition between local authorities and distorted teaching goals. In Germany too, there is a reluctance to implement national testing for fear of undesirable side effects. The German *Länder* do have in common with most other European countries, however, the existence of state inspectorates which in practice have an important role in setting and monitoring standards in those countries. At the federal level, procedures exist for ensuring comparability of *abitur* and teacher education standards between *Länder*. This process has recently been complicated by the inclusion of the former East German *Länder*.

Outcomes-oriented Standards

Most of the countries participating in the study are moving towards goals or outcomes-oriented standards. This move is usually associated with the introduction or revision of a National Curriculum or National Curriculum guidelines, which often include benchmarks of desired student performance at key stages. Some countries with long-standing traditions of centralized curriculum planning are moving towards giving schools greater autonomy, associated with a concern for quality in student learning outcomes. The definition of standards becomes difficult as one gets into the detail (and this shows up nicely the difficulties of international comparisons). The Swedish expert claimed that the term had no equivalent until recently in Sweden but was now being introduced in a confusing way to mean different things. Generally, performance standards refer either to specific *a priori* criteria of student performance or alternatively to the attainments of students in high stakes examinations. Often there is a difference of approach to the setting and monitoring of standards in the National Curriculum and in the final secondary examinations, especially where the latter are high stakes selection examinations for entry to universities.

One other major difference emerged between those countries which have a strong tradition of standard-setting at the end of secondary school based on national examinations of curriculum mastery in a range of subjects (Germany, France, Spain, UK), and those where standardized psychometric testing is the norm (notably the US). The latter may in fact be fairer in terms of discrimination between students on the basis of potential for further study but non-curriculum based psychometric tests do not have the same impact on students and teachers in reinforcing normative standards as the *abitur* or the *baccalaureate*, for example. American researchers and policy-makers are increasingly aware of this difference and many are convinced that it is part of the explanation for the contrast in standards in the upper secondary school which they perceive between their system and those with which they compare it.

It is in France and the UK that the most far-reaching developments have occurred in national testing. However the aims of the French tests diverge somewhat from those which have shaped developments in Britain. Testing occurs within the French system, with co-operation from the teachers' unions, at three key stages: at 8, 11 and 14 years of age. The tests take place at the beginning of the school year. The purpose is mainly diagnostic and pedagogical: to provide teachers with objective tools for evaluating the strengths and weaknesses of their students at the beginning of key stages. The tests are based on the National Curriculum and enable teachers to view the performance of their students against national standards. They are made available to students and their parents. At the system level, however, these national assessments are part of the accountability process and aggregations and analyses of the results are made at both national and regional (but not at school) level. Since last year these outcome indicators are published annually in the *Géographie de l'Ecole*. Currently, the *Département de l'Evaluation et de la Prospective* (DEP) which produces these analyses, is looking at ways of comparing school results using a value-added approach. In Britain, national testing at key stages has not received the full support of teachers because it is thought that the principal purpose is to grade (and potentially to reward or punish) schools and teachers, on the basis of their students' performance. The publication of test results at school level is linked with the encouragement of parental choice of schools.

Setting Performance Standards

Interest in setting performance standards, other than at terminal secondary level, is a very recent development in most of the countries surveyed. The Australian expert reported that Australian states are attempting to marry curriculum and psychometric considerations in establishing their new assessment systems. National Curriculum profiles include *a priori* standards to be achieved, expressed as desirable learning outcomes. These are not binding on States but have been influential. In some States, however, monitoring of actual student performance has led to an *a posteriori* redefinition of standards. The reformed Spanish system establishes National Curriculum guidelines in core subjects, including attainment targets, but leaves the establishment of actual assessment procedures and standards to schools. The English system has the most detailed arrangements for setting and monitoring standards and is the only one currently proposing to evaluate schools on the basis of students' performance against these standards. By contrast, the German *Länder* have quite deliberately decided not to go down this road. Apart from the *Abitur*, external evaluation, centralized testing and large-scale assessments play no decisive role in Germany when it comes to formulating and monitoring standards. Instead there is at work a 'systemic network' which underpins standards. This system is based on curriculum guidelines to which text books have to conform and to the teacher training and inspection procedures which ensure a common understanding among teachers and the public of what standards are. A similar system operates in Japan where the course of study laid down by Monbusho, combined with control of textbooks and of teacher training, together are considered sufficient guarantee of standards.

Conclusion

Overall, what emerges is a picture of some convergence between those systems which formerly constrained teachers within a straitjacket of regulations and tightly controlled procedures but which are now relaxing these restraints and giving teachers more autonomy, and those previously decentralized systems, especially in the English-speaking world, which are now tightening their curricular and assessment procedures. Interestingly, both groups of countries cite international comparisons and the need to prepare their students to compete in the high-tech world as reasons for these changes. Those countries where accountability pressures are less clamorous, notably Germany and Japan, are relatively confident about standards and there is apparently little demand from politicians or the public for evidence of student performance. In these countries, and others such as Spain, there are no national tests. However, high stakes terminal secondary examinations in Germany and Spain and competition for entry to prestigious universities in Japan probably have a 'backwash effect' on standards throughout the school system. In other countries national testing is seen as a necessary component of accountability in a democratic political system. The paradox is that too much prescription of content and performance standards, especially when linked with high-profile reporting of test results, may damage teacher professionalism. Yet it is the high professional status and public esteem of teachers which seems to characterize those countries where student performance standards are highest.

2 Assessment Styles in the Home Countries

Wynne Harlen

Summary

The first section of this chapter sets out briefly the arrangements and significant differences within them for testing in England, Wales, Scotland and Northern Ireland in 1993–4. It is important to specify the date since changes in some countries are frequent events. The second section takes three themes, of teachers' assessment, test and moderation, and compares them across the countries and the third section deals with some of the issues emerging.

Introduction

In the first announcement of the intention to introduce national statements on the curriculum and on assessment it was acknowledged that these would take different forms in the countries within the United Kingdom (UK). The main differences have been among Scotland, Northern Ireland and England; differences between England and Wales have been related mainly to provision for the Welsh language. The intention to 'introduce legislation . . . to provide for a National Curriculum in maintained schools' (DES/WO, 1987) was clear in the opening statement of the consultation document in England and Wales, whilst the equivalent document in Scotland proposed 'a programme of clarification and definition rather than of fundamental changes' (SED, 1987) which would aim to supply teachers with 'adequate guidance' on matters relating to the curriculum and assessment. Not only were there differences in the structure and legal status of the written curriculum but different arrangements for assessment and testing have also had a marked impact on the interpretation and implementation of the curriculum.

Such differences were to be expected if there was to be any attempt to acknowledge, and provide for some continuity with, the curricular and assessment practices in the different countries in the years before 1987. The traditions and historically determined social contexts of each country would naturally affect not only the position from which any changes took place, but the acceptability of changes in certain directions.

Significant Differences in National Assessment Arrangements within the UK

The initial proposals for assessment and testing in England, Scotland and Northern Ireland were different in several respects and were described by Harlen *et al.* (in Broadfoot *et al.*, 1992). Since that time the arrangements have been substantially changed in all three countries. In England this was due to the major revision brought about by the Dearing Review (Dearing, 1993). In Northern Ireland it followed the reports of the Review Groups for Key Stages 2 and 3 set up by NISEAC in 1993. In Scotland changes in testing only were introduced as a result of consultation in 1992 and were implemented in 1993 for primary schools and 1994 for secondary schools. In all three countries the withdrawal of cooperation by teachers and in some cases, parents, indicating severe discontent with the initial arrangements, played a part in bringing about the official reviews.

England and Wales

In the school year 1993/4 the requirement was for reported assessment at the end of each key stage: Key Stages 1, 2 and 3, ages 7, 11 and 14, with the GCSE examination continuing to cater for the 14–16 age group. For pupils at the end of the first three key stages teachers were required to make, or rather draw together, their own assessments across the three core subjects of the National Curriculum. In addition, in May or June of the summer term these pupils were required to take standard tasks or standards tests covering some attainment targets of the core subjects.

Reporting to parents was in terms of levels at the end of the key stages but not at other times. Reporting on other subjects outside the core was at teachers' discretion. Schools were required to send their test data to the Local Education Authority so that, at some future date, league tables of schools performance may be produced at age 11 and 16. Teachers were required to carry out the testing and to report it to parents with their own assessments.

Moderation has been a key feature of Key Stage 1 assessment since 1992. By 1994 the term 'moderation' was dropped in favour of 'audit moderation' or 'verification', thus indicating a move away from professional development and decision making towards a regulatory model of checking up on the outcomes of assessment.

Scotland

Neither the curriculum, called the 5–14 development programme, nor the assessment and testing arrangements are mandatory in Scotland, however the tradition of following central advice means that all schools have declared themselves at least intending to use them. There is no equivalent of 'key stages' in the Scottish curriculum and assessment, nor is the terminology of years 1–12 used. There are seven years in the primary school, P1 to P7, and the compulsory years of the secondary school are S1 to S4, but the 5–14 curriculum applies only up to S2.

Up to 1994 attainment targets for pupils aged 5 to 14 were specified in the curriculum at 5 levels; a proposal to add a sixth level at the top had yet to be implemented. Teachers are expected gradually to use the terminology of levels and targets in their own assessments and in reporting to parents for all pupils at first in English and mathematics (by the end of 1994/5) and for other subject areas by degrees until full implementation of the curriculum and assessment in 1998/9.

Arrangements for testing in operation in 1994 required all pupils in P1 to P7 and in S1 and S2 to take tests in reading, writing and mathematics when their teacher's own assessment indicated that they were ready to do so. Test results for individual pupils were included in reports to parents and, for the school as a whole, to the School Boards. There has never been any central collection of test data, thus no league tables of schools' performance can be produced. Nonetheless the shadow of league tables, from south of the border, was responsible for much of the resistance to testing which has persisted in some schools and education authorities. The tests are described as serving to 'provide teachers with the means to check their own assessments and ensure more consistent interpretation by teachers of what particular levels of attainment mean' (SOED, 1992). In this way they are presented as a procedure for quality assurance in relation to teachers' assessments. Apart from the regular checking by the Scottish Examination Board of the marking of a small sample of tests, no other moderation procedures have been suggested.

Northern Ireland

The statutory curriculum sets out statement of attainment targets at 10 levels for pupils aged 5 to 16. Revised arrangements for assessment and testing introduced in 1993 required teachers to carry out their own assessment of all pupils but to report in terms of levels only at the end of Key Stages 1, 2 and 3 (years 4, 7 and 10). To help teachers with their assessments two types of materials have been published by the Northern Ireland Council for the Curriculum, Examinations and Assessment (CCEA). One of these, External Assessment Resources (EARs), consists of tasks which can be incorporated into normal classwork and which help teachers to arrive at judgments expressed in terms of levels. The second type, known as 'assessment units', takes the form of short 20-minute tests in English and mathematics (for Key Stages 1, 2 and 3) and in science (for Key Stage 3 only). They have the following characteristics:

- a compulsory part of the 1993/4 pilot assessment arrangements;
- contribute both to formative and summative assessment;

- designed to help a teacher confirm an assessment of a pupil's progress in an attainment target;
- may be preceded by preparatory classroom work;
- require individual work by a pupil;
- must be used during the final two terms of the key stages but at a time chosen by the teacher;
- eventually to be made available to teachers of all years (NISEAC, 1993).

There are also Common Assessment Instruments (CAIs) which are formal tests, marked by teachers. These were used at the end of Key Stages 2 and 3 on a pilot trial basis in 1992 and 1993, but their compulsory use was then suspended whilst the impact of the new assessment units was evaluated. The possibility remains of their reintroduction at some future date.

Schools are required to report to the CCEA the end of key stage results for each pupil in each attainment target and it is intended that, after the pilot years, league tables will be published based on Key Stage 2 results.

Moderation procedures have played a major role in the assessment arrangements in Northern Ireland. In 1993/4 the emphasis shifted to quality assurance; the previous individual pupil moderation was removed and teachers of pupils at the end of Key Stages 1, 2 and 3 were required to take part in agreement trialling, where groups of teachers consider pupils' work with the intention of standardizing their judgments. Schools were also required to create a portfolio of samples of assessed work which was submitted to the CCEA, which was 'to illustrate the process of assessment in the school as a whole and separate samples will not be required for each teacher in the school' (NISEAC, 1993). These were used in conjunction with the record of the schools' end of key stage assessments by the CCEA to identify schools where some adjustment may be needed to the assessments being made.

Themes

Having reviewed the formal requirements, this section looks at what seems to be happening in practice in various aspects of National Curriculum assessment and testing, using material from evaluation studies.

Teachers' Assessments

In all countries it is intended that teachers should be assessing the progress of their pupils at all stages against the descriptions or statements of attainment at each level. In general the way in which they do this, and record it, has been a matter for the individual teachers or schools to decide. In all cases, also, there is an expectation that summative teachers' assessments are reported at certain points in terms of levels. Just how teachers make their ongoing assessments and how (or indeed if) they use them in their teaching and how (or, again, if) they use them in producing summative assessments for the end of year or end of key stage, has been extremely difficult to research. Some of the reasons include:

- the tendency of teachers to equate assessment with testing;
- the tendency of teachers to equate assessment with recording (leading many to go 'over the top' on devising time-consuming recording procedures);
- the intuitive nature of many of their judgments ('a teacher just knows her children');
- practice is highly embedded in actions, which are not analyzed by teachers and which they cannot articulate.

The help provided for teachers has varied. In Scotland the national guidelines *Assessment 5–14*, published in final form October 1991, firmly underline assessment 'as an important and integral part of the learning and teaching process' (SOED, 1991, p. 4). These guidelines are concerned only with assessment by teachers as part of ongoing work. There is an accompanying staff development pack, made available to headteachers, which provides examples and further detail to assist the translation of the guidelines into practice.

The impact of these guidelines appeared only very slowly. In a questionnaire survey carried out by the evaluation project in November 1992, a year after the publication of the guidelines, one third of primary teachers indicated that they had not read them in sufficient depth to form a view about them. The slow take-off could be explained by several factors. First, that teachers' prime concerns were with the curriculum guidelines, particularly in English and mathematics. Second, that in 1991 and 1992 testing was compulsory and there was a national campaign against it. Assessment was inevitably seen as part of the same process. Third, that in many teachers' minds, continuous assessment was synonymous with continuous recording which many teacher resisted as being too time-consuming.

A further point is that more specific help with implementing assessment as part of teaching had been promised for some time, but was published only late in 1994. This takes the form of packs of materials to help with diagnostic assessment, published under the title 'Taking a Closer Look' (SCRE, 1994). A feature of this material is its explicit indication of possible 'next steps' for children who have, and for those who have not, achieved certain levels of skill or understanding.

In Northern Ireland, the production of External Assessment Resources (EARs) was given priority and quantities of these materials, in English, mathematics and science, intended to be used as part of ongoing work, were made available to teachers. Although the EARs claim to have a formative function, they have much less explicit help in the matter of action to take than the

Scottish diagnostic assessment materials. In 1992/3 55 per cent of Key Stage 2 teachers used EARs and found them useful. But there was a distinct reduction in the use of EARs during the 1993/4 pilot year, with less than a third of both Key Stage 1 and Key Stage 2 teachers making use of them. At Key Stage 3 about half of teachers made use of EARs and a high proportion found them useful. Indeed, there is no evidence that the EARs are not seen as potentially useful material but the introduction of mandatory assessment units did not, at least in the initial stages, encourage their use.

In England, and in Northern Ireland, training has been provided for teachers, focusing mainly on end-of-key stage teachers and their particular obligations, thus emphasizing reporting and testing arrangements. In both countries these sessions have featured 'agreement trialling' and a study of examples of assessed work published by the School Examination and Assessment Council (SEAC, 1993) and by NISEAC. Although discussion of children's work has proved effective in providing operational examples of the meaning of statements of attainment, they have been found to have disadvantages. In Northern Ireland teachers gained the impression that 'agreement' meant 'agreement with the judgments made by NISEAC', who had produced the examples of assessed work. As a result many felt less confidence in own judgments (D'Arcy *et al.*, 1994). However, when teachers bring their own pupils' work to discuss, other problems have been revealed. The observation recorded in England by James included the following:

- Some tasks did not appear to provide the appropriate opportunities for children to demonstrate the attainment target being assessed; or, an attempt to embed the task in a topic may have confused children by drawing their attention to contextual details not strictly relevant to the assessment;

- Some teachers appeared to be assessing an attainment target other than the one they claimed to be assessing;

- Teachers' observations were largely judgments. The teachers providing these samples often appeared to lack a concept of evidence in terms of recording what children actually did or said;

- There was no evidence of any diagnostic or formative element in many of the samples of teacher assessments;

- Many of the assessment tasks did not appear to challenge children; they tended to be boring or 'safe'.
  (James, 1994b)

These are worrying findings, indicating that teachers need a great deal of help with the process of formative assessment.

Tests

Testing in Scotland differs from the rest of the UK by being:

- not compulsory;
- carried out at a time when teachers decide;
- not reported centrally;
- intended to enable teachers to check their own assessments.

The new arrangements (SEB, 1993a; SEB, 1993b) were implemented in Scotland in primary schools from January 1993 and in secondary schools from January 1994. The evaluation interviews with primary teachers early in the spring term of 1994, indicated that only twenty of the 135 interviewed had carried out any testing, although 82 per cent of schools were claiming to be using the tests. This anomaly might be explained by the preference of teachers to wait to carry out testing until the second half of the school year, when they would know their pupils better. It is also important not to under-estimate the demands of the procedures, which are much greater than just receiving tests through the post and following instructions. In a primary school, for example, the decision of all teachers in the school as to which children are ready for testing and which of the choice of test units in the catalogue is appropriate for each one, have to be collated. Test units then have to be ordered, the availability of the required resources checked, before the tests are used and marked.

Initial reactions to the testing arrangements introduced in 1993 and 1994 in Scotland indicated reluctant acceptance, with teachers preferring the flexible use to the previous requirement to test all P4 and P7 children within a certain period, but criticism of their time-consuming nature. The comments of teachers and headteachers also reflected the tests being criticized for failing to fulfil a role that they were no longer intended to have. That is, they were not intended primarily to provide information about pupils but to provide information about teachers' assessments. Their intended role, for moderation, seemed to be recognized by a relatively small proportion of headteachers. Other evaluation findings suggested that this was not because headteachers saw no need for moderation. Evidence from interviews suggests that schools were beginning, often in collaboration with other schools if a cluster organization existed, to set up banks of exemplars of assessed work or to hold meetings to discuss assessment of particular pieces of work in order to align judgments made by teachers in their own assessments. At the same time some teachers were beginning to realize that the tests were useful in coming to terms with the meaning of levels.

The comments made by teachers, although critical, did at least indicate that teachers were making their own assessments of pupils and that they were basing their orders for test units on their own assessments of the children's abilities. By contrast, in Northern Ireland, where the assessment units in 1993/4 had a similar role in relation to teachers' assessments at the end of the key stages, it was clear that many teachers did not have the confidence to make their own assessments of pupils' levels, or did not realize the need to do so, and used other strategies. A substantial proportion used the assessment unit material itself as the basis of determining the pupils' levels of working rather than the prior judgment of the teacher. In these cases the assessment units were not being used to confirm teachers' assessments, as was intended. 'Blanket testing', meaning that all pupils in the class were given the same assessment units, was indeed quite prevalent at Key Stage 3 and was not unusual at the earlier stages.

It is likely that some of the problems were unique to the first year of these arrangements, where there is no baseline to work from, but the reverence with which tests are treated must also have played some part. There is no doubt that in Northern Ireland primary schools the most important assessment is the secondary school selection examination and the end of Key Stage 2 assessment seems a pointless exercise. Further, the requirement to report all results to CCEA raises the possibility of their use for league tables and hence raises the stakes. Whenever stakes are raised, there is a preference for 'hard' data (which traditionally tests are assumed to give) over the 'soft' data from teachers' assessments.

Quality Assurance and Control (Moderation) Procedures

Some of the procedures already described as part of training and indeed the tests in Scotland and assessment units in Northern Ireland, have a role in quality assurance. The full list of procedures in England is quite extensive and includes:

- training, and in some LEAs, 'helplines';
- agreement trials both at school and LEA level;
- resource banks of assessment tasks as well as assessed work;
- school visits by moderators;
- school portfolios of evidence of teachers' judgments of children's work.

The need to provide evidence of their judgments for inspection by visiting moderators at first led schools to create individual pupil portfolios of work, which sometimes reached mammoth proportions. This hoarding defeated its own purposes — there was too much for any of the material to be accessible — and teachers have recently realized that a few well chosen, annotated pieces of work form a better basis for showing that assessment has been carried out competently, and also provides a basis for discussion with parents (James, 1994a).

Visits of moderators to primary schools in England have been reduced as a result of the change in the standard tests/tasks, which are now mainly paper and pencil tests whose administration is non-problematic. Moderators now have to visit to carry out a quality audit, mainly concerned with the consistency of teachers' assessment and standard test scripts for a sample of pupils. How long such costly practices can be sustained is a matter for conjecture. But when league tables are published based on end of Key Stage 2 results (and can be created locally from information given in school prospectuses at other key stages) there is likely to be demand for visible moderation procedures.

The problem of hoarding evidence was also encountered in Northern Ireland in 1992/3, when the role of moderators included visiting schools to ensure that assessment criteria were being uniformly applied. Teachers were worried that they would have to defend their judgments and retained almost everything a child produced, particularly class tests and 'harder' evidence of that kind. To prevent this unproductive use of time and energy, the arrangements for 1993/4 excluded individual pupil moderation. Instead schools were required to provide a folder containing a specified number of samples of work at various levels in English and mathematics. However this intended simplification did not much reduce the unmanageability of moderation for schools. The evaluation revealed considerable uncertainty about the purpose of the school folder. Many teachers appeared to be concerned that the selected work should be fair to the pupils or fair to the school, indicating that they saw it either as a form of individual pupil moderation, or an assessment of the schools' performance, rather than a check on the application of the criteria. Such misperceptions are understandable given that in the previous year moderation of individual pupil work had been part of the arrangements and the persisting prospect of league tables based on pupils' performance. Nevertheless the effect was that teachers set pupils special work to go into the folder, often worksheets or tests designed to assess specified levels. Moreover they were spending many hours selecting work across the school. The process was far more difficult and time-consuming than it was at first thought to be and some procedures being used invalidated the sample for its intended purpose.

In Scotland, in sharp contrast, no moderation procedures of these kinds have been proposed. Procedures depending on looking for patterns across schools would require central collection of assessment and this has never been envisaged. The Scottish Examination Board collects a small sample of test scripts to check on marking in order to ensure that test units are providing the information for teachers.

Issues

The Impact of Assessment on Teaching

Assessment is intended to affect teaching, thus we need to examine positive and negative effects. In all three countries there is evidence of greater attention in teaching to what is assessed. In Scotland, evidence from the evaluation, suggests that the changes taking place are such that assessment is:

- being included in lesson planning more than before;
- being carried out in the classroom more consciously;
- encompassing a wider range of learning outcomes;
- taking place within a school-wide framework;
- more often than before recorded in a structured manner.
  (Harlen *et al.*, 1995)

Teachers report more attention to some aspects which were previously neglected in assessment and teaching; these include listening and speaking in English, problem solving in mathematics and in some cases, creativity. Thus the effect of the assessment arrangements appeared to be to extend rather than to narrow the range of work included and assessed. At the same time there is some evidence of teachers including more formal assessment in their work, perhaps in response to the need to show in their programme planning how they are assessing the attainment targets they are working towards. However, the evidence that teachers use is mainly from observing, discussing and marking work.

In Northern Ireland it is hard to avoid the impression that rather than assessment being part of teaching, the main activity is assessing, from which hopefully children learn something. Teachers have been asked to operate and elaborate time-consuming procedures which have inevitably separated assessment from teaching in their minds. Indeed the impression has been given that assessment is all about collecting evidence, and the 'harder' the better. Thus they have turned their own teachers' assessment into a series of teacher-made tests. 'In such a climate the idea of assessment being part of teaching, involving pupils and leading to appropriate action flies out the window' (D'Arcy, Curry and Harlen, 1993).

There is also the issue of teaching to the tests. In Northern Ireland, the 1993/4 assessment arrangements, quoted earlier, indicate that assessment units 'may be preceded by preparatory classroom work'. This not only seems to have been taken by some teachers as an invitation to 'teach and then test' but clouds the message about the role of assessment units. If the assessment units are intended essentially to confirm teachers' assessments, then it would be expected that all the material in the programme of study for the particular stage had been covered at the level where a pupil was judged to be operating. However, if the assessment units are regarded as having a more independent role then this might be seen to justify special preparation for them. In the Northern Ireland context, where the publication of results is in the front of teachers' minds, the apparently 'hard' data provided by assessment units is likely to tip the balance towards the assumption of an independent role. In England, James (1994b) found evidence of coaching for standard tests from moderators who had 'observed teaching in the morning of the material to be tested through SATs in the afternoon' and she quotes a moderator's view that rising levels of results in National Curriculum assessment might be at the expense of lower real standards of education because children were being coached on a narrow range of activities.

The Balance of Formative and Summative Purposes

The developing theory of educational assessment, and various models within it particularly of formative assessment and ipsative assessment, emphasizes the important role that pupils have to play in their own assessment, as they come to understand the evaluation process, to learn to work towards explicit criteria or targets and to modify their performance in relation to constructive task-related feedback from teachers (Gipps, 1994).

In Scotland, pupil involvement is explicitly encouraged (SOED, 1991, p. 13, SOED, 1993a, p. 100), and the evaluation indicated that in 1992 seven out of ten teachers claimed to have involved pupils in assessment. In the majority of cases this took the form of an informal discussion in which pupils were encouraged to give an opinion of what they had done but it also included more formal procedures such as asking pupils to choose 'best pieces' of work to put in a folder or bag.

In England and Northern Ireland the pupil's role is rarely mentioned by teachers in their practice or in any of the documents relating to national assessment. Indeed, the reduction in use of EARs in Northern Ireland and the amount of energy and resources devoted to moderation of summative assessment and testing in England suggest that genuine formative assessment in these countries is being stifled by concern for summative assessment.

The Impact of Raising the Stakes

It is clear that in England and Wales and in Northern Ireland the national assessment stakes have been raised by the use of results for purposes which have consequences for teachers and schools. I have argued elsewhere (Harlen, 1994, p. 6) that when the stakes are raised either for pupils or teachers, quality control takes precedence over quality assurance. The latter, which aims to improve the process of assessment through professional development, assumes a high priority only when stakes are low. Thus the argument that the most appropriate ways to make teachers' assessments more dependable is through in-school and inter-school in-service and the provision of support materials, seems to be losing ground in England and Wales to a quality control model where concern is with the outcomes of tests. The external audit of Key Stage 1 tests combined with the end of mandatory audit of teacher assessment points in this direction.

Conclusion

Perhaps the most important issue emerging from this review of styles of national assessment and testing and of current practice concerns the role of teachers' classroom assessments in the provision of information for different purposes. The evaluation studies have shown that teachers' intuitive assessments do not match up to the requirements for systematic, rigorous and reliable assessments required for making fair comparisons between pupils or schools. Whether this could ever happen if more attention and resources were to be given to helping with the process of formative assessment in its full meaning is not known. What is clear, however, is that teachers' assessments are being devalued because they are less dependable than other forms of assessment. If we wish to avoid this situation and to ensure that classroom assessment plays its full role in improving teaching and learning, we might heed the argument of Stiggins (1992) who proposes a sharp separation between classroom assessment and large-scale assessment for summative and evaluative purposes, maintaining a link through the specification of the curriculum outcomes. If we do this, he argues, then teachers' lack of assessment training and rigour would matter much less if classroom and centralized assessment are kept separate, and he goes on 'prepare teachers to assess well, let their assessments serve to promote ongoing student development, and randomly sample student performance periodically with independent assessments to assure the public that schools are in fact doing the job they are supposed to do'. A similar separation between assessment for different purposes was proposed by Harlen *et al.* (1992). The nearest we have to this situation in the home countries is in Scotland, where, significantly, national monitoring by the Assessment of Achievement Programme is still in operation and where teachers' classroom assessments are not collected centrally.

References

D'Arcy, J., Curry, C. and Harlen, W. (1994) *An Evaluation of the Pilot Assessment Arrangements at Key Stages 2 and 3 in 1992–3*, Belfast, Northern Ireland Schools Examinations and Assessment Council.

D'Arcy, J., Curry, C. and Harlen, W. (1994) *An Evaluation of the Pilot Assessment Arrangements at Key Stages 1, 2 and 3 in 1993–4*, Belfast, Northern Ireland Schools Examinations and Assessment Council.

Dearing, R. (1993) *The National Curriculum and its Assessment: Final Report*, London, SCAA.

Gipps, C. (1994) *Beyond Testing: Towards a Theory of Educational Assessment*, London, Falmer Press.

Harlen, W. (1994) 'Introduction', in Harlen, W. (Ed) *Enhancing Quality in Assessment*, London, Paul Chapman Publishing.

Harlen, W., Broadfoot, P., Brown, S., Dockrell, B., Gipps, C. and Nuttall, D. (1992) 'A comparison of the proposals for national assessment in England, Wales, Scotland and Northern Ireland', in Broadfoot, P. *et al.* (Eds) *Policy Issues in National Assessment*, BERA Dialogues No 7, Clevedon, Multilingual Matters.

HARLEN, W., GIPPS, C., BROADFOOT, P. and NUTTALL, D. (1992) 'Assessment and the improvement of education', *The Curriculum Journal*, **3**, 3, pp. 215–230.

HARLEN, W., MALCOLM, H. and BYRNE, M. (1994) 'Teachers' assessment and national testing in primary schools in Scotland: Roles and relationships', *Assessment in Education*, in press.

JAMES, M. (1994a) 'Experience of quality assurance at Key Stage 1', in HARLEN, W. (Ed) *Enhancing Quality in Assessment*, London, Paul Chapman Publishing.

JAMES, M. (1994b) 'Teachers' assessment and national testing in England: Roles and relationships', Paper presented at the British Educational Research Association Annual Conference, Oxford, September 1994.

NISEAC (1993) *Guide to the Pilot Assessment Arrangements: Key Stages 1 and 2 1994*, Belfast, Northern Ireland Schools Examinations and Assessment Council.

SEAC (1993) *Children's Work Assessed* (*KS1*) and *Pupils' Work Assessed* (*KS2*), London, Schools Examination and Assessment Council.

SEB (1993a) *The Framework for National Testing*, 5–14 Assessment Unit, Scottish Examination Board.

SEB (1993b) *Assessment 5–14: A Teacher's Guide to National Testing in Primary Schools*, 5–14 Assessment Unit, Scottish Examination Board.

SCRE (1994) *Taking a Closer Look at Mathematics. Taking a Closer Look at English. Taking a Closer Look at Science*, Edinburgh, Scottish Council for Research in Education.

SOED (1991) *Assessment 5–14 National Guidelines*, Edinburgh, SOED.

SOED (1992) *Arrangements for National Testing*, circular 12/92, Edinburgh, SOED.

SOED (1994) *Implementing 5–14: A Progress Report*, Interchange No 23, Edinburgh, Research and Intelligence Unit, SOED.

STIGGINS, R.J. (1992) 'Two disciplines of educational assessment', Paper presented at the States Assessment Conference, Bolder, June 1992 and published in *Evaluation and Development*.

3 Ensuring Comparability of Standards in the International Baccalaureate

Ian W. Walker

Summary

Given both the position of the International Baccalaureate (IB) in the educational marketplace, and the structure of the IB Diploma programme, the issue of 'Comparability of standards' is of major importance to the organization. In the main, the IB uses similar approaches to tackle this problem as are used elsewhere in the world.

However, not only does the IB Diploma programme contain certain features which if not unique, are certainly not common to other educational programmes, but also, the IB candidate population is distinctly different in a number of ways to those normally encountered in national educational systems.

These two general characteristics pose a number of challenges to the IB assessment and grading systems which require particular solutions if IB standards are to be applied and then maintained in a consistent manner. Furthermore, they also have a major bearing on the issue of comparability of these standards.

Introduction

In order to understand the challenges faced by the IB it is therefore important to understand the nature of the IB Diploma programme and the candidates who follow it.

The International Baccalaureate Organisation (IBO) provides a Diploma programme which is an international pre-university curriculum and an internationally recognized university entry qualification. The programme is often represented in diagrammatic form as a hexagon (see Figure 3.1 below). As you can see from the figure, candidates must study six subjects, of which at least one of these subjects must be chosen from each of Groups 1–5. All subjects can be studied at either Higher or Subsidiary Level; candidates are required to study three subjects at Higher level and three subjects at Subsidiary Level. In addition to qualify for the Diploma, candidates must follow a course in Theory

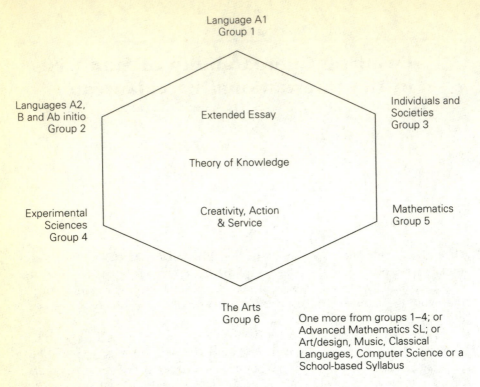

Figure 3.1:   *The International Baccalaureate Diploma*

of Knowledge, submit an Extended Essay, and take part in Creativity, Action and Service (CAS).

Subjects are graded on a 1 (poor) to 7 (excellent) point scale, and a total of 3 bonus points are available for performance on the Extended Essay and in Theory of Knowledge. Twenty-four points are required for the award of the Diploma.

The curriculum is designed to be international, innovative and balanced. It is important to note that the IB Diploma programme aims to be truly international in all aspects of its curriculum and assessment. It is not merely a nationally based programme such as A-levels or AP which is available around the world.

Availability

The IB is only available in schools authorized by the Organization to offer the programme. To some extent this is a factor which allows some small measure of control over the candidate population. However, this effect is small since IB does not have any control over the way schools deliver the programme.

Growth in demand for the IB has, in recent years, been steady at around 12 per cent per annum, made up both of new schools joining as well as established IB schools entering greater numbers of candidates. This growth is not however homogenous, but is greater in some areas of the world than in others. In recent years growth has been noticeable in Eastern Europe — there are now IB schools in Hungary, Czechoslovakia, Poland, Slovenia, Croatia and Russia — in Finland, as well as in Australia and Latin America. Currently, significant interest is shown in China, South Africa and Scotland.

All in all, the IB is now available in over 550 schools in over seventy countries worldwide. Nowadays, these schools are of many different types, e.g. international schools, state schools, private schools, and so on. The Diploma is accepted worldwide by over 800 universities in over eighty countries as satisfying national matriculation requirements for university entrance. Offers may be made on the basis of the total points score achieved by the candidate or on the basis of performance in certain subjects.

Many countries have created 'equivalence formulae' in order to compare IB results with those of their national qualification. As yet, however, IBO has not endorsed any such formulae since the two programmes being compared are usually too dissimilar for meaningful comparisons to be made.

Unlike the early years of the IB when the demand was mainly due to the international portability of the curriculum and the Diploma, nowadays, it is the quality of the curriculum and the level of academic standards implicit in the award of the IB Diploma which are the major factors behind the increasing demand for the programme. This is borne out by some recent research which confirms this view, at least from the perspective of the schools which currently offer the programme.

International Currency

In some cases, the international currency of the Diploma in both curricula and assessment terms, facilitates the international mobility of students to universities in other countries. In other cases, schools, parents and others may be dissatisfied with the curriculum and/or standards available through the national programme and therefore opt, at some additional cost, to adopt the IB programme.

To some extent, this latter reason may explain the recent interest in the IB in certain Australian states, where there is concern over academic standards. In curricular terms it may also explain the interest in the United Kingdom (UK) where it is seen as a broader curriculum compared to A-levels.

The high quality of the curriculum and standards are crucial to the IBO. It should not be forgotten that unlike national educational systems, the IB has no guaranteed market. It always exists as an alternative to the nationally available programme and therefore it has no choice but to offer a high quality programme. In this respect, comparability of standards is as essential as high standards themselves.

However, the steady growth makes the maintenance of standards an on-going challenge. Growth brings with it both opportunities and challenges. Not only is the growth non-homogenous simply in terms of the distribution of schools and candidates, but also in terms of their demands. Furthermore, the nature of the IB programme, the cultural variety of its candidature, the variety of options it offers — such as the wide choice of languages — the unique features such as Theory of Knowledge and the Extended Essay, and the availability of three working languages do not make the task any easier.

Partnership and Transparency

The IB attempts to overcome these inherent challenges by using various generic strategies, in particular those of partnership and transparency, both of which are essential for the success of international standards. IB has, furthermore, in recent years imported into the management of its activities, the idea of 'Building quality in at the beginning' and being concerned with quality in terms of continuous improvement. This approach is seen as fundamental to achieving success, given IB's position in the educational market.

Transparency ensures that all those involved in studying/teaching/assessing IB courses are as fully informed as possible concerning the requirements and expectations of the programme; the idea being that this will help eliminate significant differences and is, therefore, a step towards comparability. Thus all objectives, assessment criteria and marking schemes are made available when appropriate. Criteria of assessment are provided in each of the major domains within a subject and are illustrated by the use of achievement level descriptors. Not only does this apply in an *a priori* sense but also after the examinations, when IB is currently supplying schools with ever increasing amounts of feedback to support and explain the final grades which are issued.

The idea of partnership extends and generalizes this sharing of information between all those involved in the IB programme; teachers, examiners and staff. This occurs across all activities; curriculum development, teacher training, question setting, assessment and grade awarding. IB regularly arranges workshops around the world to allow teachers to not only meet one another but also to discuss issues of concern with senior examiners and representatives of the IBO. It also allows IB to apply the maxim of 'building quality in at the beginning' by ensuring that all views are heard and listened to in the curriculum development process, again with the aim of comparability later on.

Curriculum Development

IB Curriculum Development is managed in a participative manner, over a cycle of no more than five years, in order to keep the programme fresh in a rapidly changing world. All constituencies are represented and all those unable to attend the meetings are sent a copy of the meeting report and asked for their feedback. Everything possible is done to obtain the views of all concerned at this early part of the process.

Nowadays, most curriculum review is carried out on a by-group basis, initially devising an appropriate curriculum model and set of objectives to which subject matter can then be applied. This is the start of building in comparability at the beginning of the process.

Agreement on course content is a major challenge due to the wide variety of cultural needs to be accommodated. Narrowly defined content standards are therefore impossible to achieve in certain subjects. However, this is not seen as a problem since rather than encourage an encyclopaedic approach to learning, IB focuses on functions and abilities rather than content.

One also finds cultural differences in assessment but in order to maintain the credibility of IB standards, there is no leeway here. All students within a subject are assessed against the same criteria using the same assessment instruments. It is important to note that irrespective of geographical location or working languages, the examination papers in a subject are identical for all candidates. Similarly, all candidates are considered equivalent for the purposes of grading and the award of the Diploma.

Thus comparability with regard to a subject population is achieved by using identical assessment and grading processes based on transparent objectives and assessment criteria. Procedures are in place to ensure that as far as possible, no bias enters the system; question papers and their translations are carefully checked to ensure their validity, all original marking — which is carried out by an international team of teachers and examiners — is moderated by sampling, and final grading is carried out by teams of international examiners which will include many IB teachers.

Grading Decisions

Grading decisions are made initially on a by-component basis and are based on material evidence. IB employs a criterion referenced approach to grade awarding, the constantly shifting basis of the IB candidate population make dependence on year-by-year statistical data an unreliable process.

The group structure of the IB Diploma demands that particular care be taken with regard to ensuring equivalence of standards within a group of subjects. As previously mentioned, this is nowadays addressed right at the start of any new curriculum development by the group development approach. However, systems of assessment and grading also need to be carefully designed to eliminate as far as possible, any difference in the way candidates are treated. This is particularly a challenge in the area of languages where IB annually offers examinations in more than fifty languages at a variety of levels, for both native speakers and foreign learners. The solution has been to develop sets of assessment criteria for each of the main components of each language programme and for these to be applied and aggregated in a consistent manner.

In Language A1 (native speakers), two of the three components, World Literature and Oral work are independent of any external influence such as an examination paper. Since the same assessment criteria apply across all languages for each of these two components, the component grade boundaries for these two components are fixed for all languages. These are then aggregated with the performance on the written examination paper, not by numerical aggregation, but by employing a matrix aggregation approach. In this way, the contribution from each of the three assessment components has the same influence irrespective of the target language, thereby ensuring parity. Here again IB cannot place too much confidence in statistical comparisons since not only does the size of the candidate population across different languages vary from less than ten for some languages to thousands in others, but the internal nature of the populations is also radically different.

In the area of foreign languages, the nature of the candidate population, ranging from bilingual candidates to beginners, has meant that in the interests of equivalence IB has introduced a new suite of programmes to suit all needs. This is an example of how the rapid growth in IB has required a reaction from the organization as the needs of the candidate population have altered. However, by tackling the problem at source and hence building in the quality at the beginning by providing a more appropriate suite of programmes, it is hoped that the grades awarded will be much more appropriate and comparable than in the past. The final challenge of this development is to inform all involved of the relative merits of the grades awarded in each programme. As a step towards this we have again identified sets of assessment criteria for use in all languages to support and explain each component of each programme. Because of the additional communication problems in languages above and beyond those normally encountered in the IB, IB has developed a slightly different style of assessment criteria which it is hoped will be clearer to understand and therefore more liable to lead to consistency of assessment.

Conclusion

In conclusion, the IB Diploma programme currently enjoys steady growth around the world and the Diploma is recognized as a 'premium' educational qualification. Indeed, as an international qualification, it is now attracting competition, such as AICE from UCLES and an international certificate from AP — a sure sign of success.

Unlike national systems, the IB is not subject to governmental control, instead it is subject to market forces, since schools always have an alternative to turn to — the national offering.

Whilst this may initially appear to be a significant threat or weakness, it is in fact a major strength of the IB, since by working in partnership with its customers — schools and teachers — from the outset, it is able to update its curriculum in line with international educational developments. Furthermore, due to the international nature of its schools, IB has had to achieve international cooperation with regard to the development of curriculum, assessment and standards. It is therefore living proof that such international cooperation is possible and that as seen by the end user, the Diploma is viewed as representing standards which are considered comparable despite the many challenges faced by the IB.

4   Humanistic Education Requires Humanistic Assessment

Kari Smith

Summary

Humanistic approaches to education require humanistic assessment procedures. Learners differ, and they should be responsible for their own learning.
Learners must learn who they are.

If changes in assessment methods used in schools are to be implemented,
teachers must be familiar with these changes and believe in them.

This chapter describes how different assessment approaches are being
taught in pre- and in-service teacher training courses. The emphasis is on:

(i)   learner assessment — what is it?
(ii)   heterogeneous assessment in heterogeneous classes.
(iii) involving learners in assessment and in test-design.
(iv)   self-assessment.

The course participants experience this type of assessment in the course as
learners and discuss its application in the various cultural settings of their
teaching.

Introduction

Approaches used to appraise student progress depend on the philo-
sophy of education involved. (Ediger, 1993, p. 48)

The humanistic approach to education which places the learners in the centre
of the learning process is incorporated in a compulsory course on Evaluation,
Assessment and Testing in pre- and in-service training programmes for teachers
of English as a foreign language at Oranim School of Education of the Kibbutz
Movement in Israel. The course syllabus includes the basic theory on the topic
and relates it to the practical aspects in the classroom. The participants experience the assessment approach as students; they are involved in deciding

the assessment criteria, writing their own examinations, assessing and grading themselves at the end of the course.

In order to help teachers make effective use of evaluation, assessment, and testing in the foreign language classroom it is necessary to clarify what the concepts stand for by providing clear definitions. The definitions given below serve as the basis for this and they have been found to be of great value while working with teachers on the subject.

Evaluation is the widest basis for collecting information in the educational system. It is, according to Brindley (1989) 'conceptualized as broader in scope, and concerned with the overall program'. In the foreign language classroom it is related to the course itself or to the textbook or manual. Nunan's definition (1990) clarifies the function of evaluation and makes it comprehensible to laymen in the field:

> Evaluation refers to the wider process of interpreting data in order to make judgments about a particular program or programs.

Assessment is part of evaluation as it is concerned with the student and with what the student does (Brindley, 1989). Broadfoot (1986) claims that assessment is evaluation of students' achievements and that there are many types of assessment; each of which is designed to allow for the best judgment of 'a student's performance in a given circumstance'. Nunan (1990) defines assessment as referring to 'the set of processes through which we make judgments about a learner's level of skills and knowledge'.

The view taken in the course is that assessment is of the learner, but not only in terms of her/his achievements and measured skills and knowledge. In the classroom, especially with school children, learner assessment usually includes additional components such as attitude, effort, personal progress. Most teachers do not always specify these components with an allotted weight, but they are usually a subjective part of the teacher's assessment of the learner.

Testing is a means to assess the learner, and thereby becomes an integrated part of assessment as well as of evaluation. Gronlund and Linn (1990) define tests as 'an instrument or systematic procedure for measuring a sample of behaviour'. Tests are to a great extent the major component in learner assessment (Smith, 1993).

Figure 4.1 illustrates and sums up the three definitions used for evaluation, assessment, and testing in this specific course. Evaluation includes the whole course, programme, and information is collected from many sources, including the learner. Assessment is related to the learner and her/his achievements, attitude, effort. Testing is part of assessment, and it deals with measuring learner achievements and samples of learned behaviour.

An additional and important point that has to be made is that all three functions can be *summative* or *formative* in nature. If the process is summative it means that the information is gathered at the end of the process in order to prove and to make decisions. The formative evaluation, assessment or testing

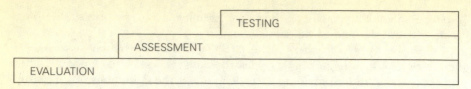

Figure 4.1: Evaluation, assessment, testing

is carried out during the process mainly in order to improve and to serve as guidance so corrections can be made (Gronlund and Linn, 1990, Rea-Dickens and Germaine, 1992). The course focuses on the formative nature of the process because that is what most classroom teachers in the school system have to work with.

Evaluation

Every school, institution, course has to be put to test at times so evaluation is a necessary function. It should be viewed as a healthy function which serves the management by providing information about the institution for ongoing improvement and decision-making. However, the individual teacher is usually not responsible for evaluation of the institution they are working for. They are, however, part of the institution and as a result they also have to be subjects of evaluation. The information about the teachers is part of the overall evaluation of the institution. The question is who the evaluators are. The learners, who are directly affected by the quality of the teachers' work, should play a major role when opinions about teachers are being formed and decisions made. The most important role of learner feedback is, however, the use the teacher can make of it in her/his own teaching. It is not always a straightforward matter for teachers to ask the learners' opinions, and many are worried it might reduce the authority they have in the class. 'How can young children say anything about my teaching?' is a comment often heard in in-service training courses. We should keep in mind, though, that the learners are directly affected by the teacher's personality, teaching techniques, skills, and knowledge, and they can provide teachers with essential information about these attributes that they may be unaware of.

There are various ways of organizing feedback from the learners; from the very informal ones such as class discussions or anonymous essay writing, to the more formal questionnaire made up for a specific class. Personally I prefer a well designed questionnaire tailored to my own teaching situation and my own class. Even young learners are capable of providing important and new information about me as a teacher and as a person they spend quite a lot of their time with.

Regardless of what method the teacher chooses in order to learn about her/his work from the pupils, it is necessary that the information is seriously dealt with and eventual changes are made. It is helpful to discuss the information with colleagues and with the learners, so confusing issues can be clarified. Teachers who have started using learner feedback as a means for their own development have reported improved relationships with their students which subsequently increased the learners' and their own motivation leading to better achievements. Unfortunately, it is not always a simple task due to teaching settings which do not allow for this type of activity and also due to feedback anxiety among the teachers. However, learners evaluate their teachers inside and outside the classroom, and it is only a question if the teacher wants to benefit from this by systematically collecting the information the learners have.

Assessment

Teachers usually feel more comfortable being the assessor of others, of learners. It is part of their job; teachers are expected to assess, to exercise the given authority. However, because it is part of the teachers' job, they have to know how to do it well, and teacher training institutions do not always provide their graduates with the necessary background, theoretical and practical, to do a good job. In a study carried out among English teachers in Israel it was found that the majority of teachers in all settings used test results as the main source for the assessment (95–100 per cent). Factors such as homework, participation and individual progress, were used mainly to round off the test results. The teachers could not specify the weight of these components (in percentage) when asked to do so (Smith, 1993).

Most assessment is reported to the learners in the form of a grade, and the question is; what does the reported grade represent? It does not matter if the grade is a letter on a scale from A to F, or in numbers from 1 to 5, or from 10 to 100. Neither does it say much more if the scale goes from *excellent* to *not satisfactory*. As long as the content behind the grade is not specified and familiar to the teacher, the pupils, and other stakeholders, the grade in itself is not very informative. Dressel (1983) has defined grades in a rather humorous way by saying:

> A grade is an inadequate report of an inaccurate judgement by a biased and variable judge of the extent to which a student has attained an undefined level of mastery of an unknown proportion of an indefinite material.

However, in addition to the humour, the above definition carries an element of truth. What does a grade reporting learner assessment really express? What information does it really provide? It is essential that the teacher decides before the assessment has to be reported, preferably at the beginning of the course, what course components are to be included in the assessment, and how much weight each component has. As soon as this is done, the pupils must be

Homework	20 per cent
Homework level	10 per cent
Participation in class	20 per cent
Individual progress	20 per cent
Tests	30 per cent
Total	100 per cent

Figure 4.2: Assessment scale (example: Israel)

Components	Weak per cent	Average per cent	Good per cent
Homework	30	20	10
Homework level	10	15	20
Participation	10	15	20
Tests	20	35	50
Individual progress	30	15	0
Total	100	100	100

Figure 4.3: Assessment scales cross section

informed about the assessment scale. It would not be realistic in this paper to suggest the best assessment scale for use in the classroom. It differs from setting to setting; depending on the course type and the age of the learners. In the Israeli school setting the following scale has been found to be useful (Figure 4.2).

Such a scale would inform the pupils that their attitude, effort and individual progress counts just as much as test results. In teaching heterogeneous classes where learners are taught at various levels it is possible to work with different scales for various groups of learners; for example see Figure 4.3 below.

The weaker pupils can be rewarded for hard work, and they are assessed according to their own progress, while the better, often more competitive pupils are mainly assessed according to external criteria against which their achievements are measured.

In any school classroom there are mixed learner populations, and we must keep in mind that all people cannot be assessed according to the same scale. School assessment should mainly be formative in nature; to improve the learner's learning and serve as motivation for future learning.

All decisions teachers make regarding assessment must be done in good time before the assessment is to be reported, and the learners need to be familiar with the scale according to which they are to be assessed. This speaks in favour of involving the learners in the assessment.

Involving Learners in the Assessment

Who says that teachers have to be the sole assessors of learners? The latter are proved to be capable assessors of themselves in the foreign language class-room. Learners self-assessment have been found to have an acceptable correlation with teacher and external assessment (Blanche, 1988; Smith, 1991), and when the many educational aspects such as increased motivation, learner responsibility and learner independence, metacognitive awareness, are also taken into consideration, there are numerous reasons in favour of involving the learners in the assessment of their own learning. If these many advantages are to be fully exploited, the assessment process needs to be systematically planned, and in the following an approach to involving learners in the assessment will be presented.

The first step is to provide the learners with the objectives of the course and with a course outline including the requirements. The learners have to know what they can expect and what is expected of them.

The second step takes place when about a third of the course has been concluded. The teacher involves the learners in a discussion of what has been taught so far in the course, and how it has been taught. The preparation can be done at home by the individual learner who is asked to go through her/his notebook and make a list for the following class when the information is elicited from the learners in a brainstorm activity. The teacher organizes the information on the board or on a transparency. This is a useful activity to make the learners review the material and fill in 'empty spots' in their note books.

The third step is done in groups of four to five pupils with the task of deciding what course components the learner assessment should consist of, what activities they should be assessed on. The lists the learners usually produce are rather conventional; they often include homework, participation, individual progress, tests, etc. In courses not related to the school system the various skills, grammar and vocabulary are often specified, together with individual progress and effort.

The fourth step consists of reporting and voting. The groups report their lists of components, the pupils vote for the one they prefer to be assessed on, and the suggestion with most votes becomes the basis for assessment in that class.

The fifth step is again carried out in groups, and this time the task is to allot a weight to each component, totalling 100 per cent (which is the system used in Israel). Once again, the groups report and vote for the proposal they feel best reflects the course work. At the end of the fifth step the class (including the teacher) have a list of components and the weight of these according to which assessment will be based. It is necessary to say (and the pupils expect this) that the teacher has a veto, and she/he can use it if necessary. In other words, the teacher has to approve of the decisions made by the class. From experience, I can say that in most cases there is usually strong agreement between the pupils' scale and what the teacher had in mind.

The sixth step is optional, but nevertheless, recommended. The learners are asked to assess themselves according to the newly created scale, and thereby they analyze their own learning based on the main components of the course. The teacher assesses the learners independently, and the average mark is calculated and used. If the discrepancy between the teacher's and the learner's assessment is 10 per cent or more, the teacher should discuss the mark with the learner in an individual tutorial. If the process is well planned this does not frequently happen. In any case, the self-assessment/teacher-assessment serves as an excellent springboard for any individual tutorial with the learners.

The main advantages of this approach to learner assessment are:

1   the assessment is based on what really takes place in the course and is therefore more likely to be valid;
2   the assessment criteria are clear to the learners and to the teacher;
3   the learners are active partners in deciding how to be assessed. This leads to increased empathy between the two parties;
4   the learners have to face their own reality as learners. They become aware of their weaknesses and strengths;
5   assessment is carried out by two raters, thereby there is possibility for increased reliability;
6   it provides a good opportunity for formative evaluation of the course in addition to formative assessment of the learners.

The disadvantages of this approach are pinpointed below to be kept in mind:

1   it is time consuming. The process will take about three to four clock hours if done properly;
2   not all learners are willing to take on responsibility, neither are all teachers strong enough to share responsibility;
3   self-assessment is not accepted in all cultures;
4   marks cannot be used for comparative purposes as each group might choose different components and scales. It is therefore recommended to be used for formative purposes during the year, and not by itself for summative purposes and certification.

Testing

Testing is the main tool teachers use in order to collect information about the learner, and test results usually serve as the main component of the grade.

There are two types of tests language learners and teachers have to deal with. The first type is the external exams required by an external body for certification purposes. These tests are designed by professional test writers and have been found to be both valid and reliable. The purpose of external tests are to provide information for summative assessment of the learner.

Few classroom teachers are involved with designing external tests. The teachers' task is to prepare their pupils for these tests, and as a result the backwash effect of external tests is noticeable in graduate classes. In this respect it can be said that external tests are used as teaching material due to the strong influence they have on what is being taught. In the course, testing for formative purposes is discussed and ways of how to use formative tests as learning material will be proposed.

Teachers usually assign a class test after a certain amount of material has been covered. In order to find out how much the class has learned from what has been taught, a progress test is designed by the teacher and its marks become a major part of learner assessment. However, the learners can also be actively involved in the test designing process and in the marking of the tests. As a result the formative tests become part of the learning material in the course. As an example the following steps are suggested:

1   the class has concluded a unit in the textbook on which the learners will be tested. The learners are asked to review the unit at home; going carefully through the textbook and their notebook in order to list what has been taught and also how it has been practised;

2   in the following class the teacher elicits the information from the learners in a brainstorming activity, trying to organize it on the board;

3   the teacher reveals some of the 'secrets' of test design to the learners; such as tests being samples of what has been taught, and no new techniques or activities are introduced in a test. It is also recommended to ensure an increased level of difficulty in the test, and that instructions have to be clear, the lay out attractive, and each item has to be given a weight;

4   in groups of four the students are asked to write a test based on the material taught and the way it was practised using the guidelines previously received;

5   the teacher collects the tests made up by the learners and designs the final version which will be taken by the pupils a week or so later. While designing the test it is important that only learners' test items are used and that each group is represented in the final version. The teacher's task is to correct the language and to see that the test is given a fair scoring key;

6   when the day of the test arrives, the pupils have had time to prepare at home. It is possible to familiarize the learners with all the test items written by various groups; this ensures a more thorough preparation and better learning of the material;

7   after the tests are written, the teacher collects and marks them, but
    nothing is written on the test-paper itself. All comments are written
    separately;

8   the test-papers are returned to the learners as they were handed in,
    but the teacher makes it quite clear that they have been corrected
    and marked;

9   in groups the learners discuss the test, trying to agree upon the cor-
    rect answers which are then reported to the class, and the correct
    version is elicited and written on the board;

10 the final step is that the learners now correct and mark their own
    tests using the key on the board. The teacher compares the pupil
    given mark to her/his mark. Usually there is strong agreement be-
    tween the two marks and in case of discrepancy the learner is often
    stricter than the teacher.

The advantages of this carefully structured approach to formative testing are
first of all that test anxiety should be reduced because the learners know they
are responsible for the test items, and they are familiar with part of, if not all,
the test. As a result motivation is often increased as the learners are eager to
see what part of their group test has been included in the final version. The
material is thoroughly reviewed; first at home while going through the material, then in class designing the test itself. In order to write a test question, the
material needs to be understood. During the preparation for the test at home
the material is once more reviewed, this time with deeper comprehension and
more interest. The group discussion of the test clarifies problems, and the self-
correction ensures revised learning of the material. That is often the time when
'real' learning takes place.

The main disadvantage of the approach is, as with the assessment approach described, time. It takes several lessons to go through the process, and
my advice is to spend less time on teaching the material, and more time on
learning the material by giving the learners meaningful tasks to work on.

Conclusion

Learner-centred teaching requires learner-centred assessment. This paper has
described how this is taught to teachers and teachers-to-be.

The feedback on the course and its impact on the participants' teaching
is encouraging, and it reflects the need for such a course in training programmes. However, above that, it is essential that policy makers examine the
assessment approaches used in education, and if we accept that learners shall
be taught at their own level of ability, that they shall play an active and
responsible role in the learning process, they must be assessed accordingly.

References

BLANCHE, P. (1988) 'Self-assessment of foreign language skills: Implications for teachers and researchers', *RELC Journal*, **19**, 1, pp. 75–93.

BRINDLEY, G. (1989) *Assessing Achievements in the Learner-centred Curriculum*, National Centre for English Language Teaching Research, Sidney, Macquarie University.

BROADFOOT, P. (Ed) (1986a) *Profiles and Records of Achievement*, London, Rinehart and Winston, London.

DRESSEL, P. (1983) 'Grades: One more tilt at the windmill' in CICKERING, A.W. (Ed) *AAHE Bulletin*, **35**, 8, pp. 10–13.

EDIGER, M. (1993) 'Approaches to measurement and evaluation', *Studies in Educational Evaluation*, **19**, 1, pp. 41–49.

GRONLUND, N.E. and LINN, R.L. (1990) *Measurement and Evaluation in Teaching*, 6th edition, New York, Macmillan.

NUNAN, D. (1990) 'Action research in the classroom' in RICHARDS, J.C. and NUNAN, D. (Eds) *Second Language Teacher Education*, Cambridge, Cambridge University Press, pp. 62–82.

REA-DICKENS, P. and GERMAINE, K. (1992) *Evaluation*, Oxford University Press.

SMITH, K. (1991) 'Correlation between teacher evaluation and students' self-evaluation in EFL', Paper presented at the EARLI conference in Turku, August.

SMITH, K. (1993) 'The assessment habits of the Israeli English teacher', Paper presented at the EARLI conference in Aix-en-Provence, September.

5 Comparison Without Comparability

Keith Drake

Summary

The verb 'to compare' means either to juxtapose or to differentiate. It implies recognition of difference between objects being compared just as much as similarity. On the other hand, 'comparable' unambiguously implies equivalence. Not surprisingly, comparison is common and comparability is much rarer. Comparison is not a matter of degree; comparability is. Whether the degree of comparability is adequate depends upon the purpose of the comparison. But even when the degree of comparability across countries is insufficient, for example to treat measures as additive, much may still be learned from comparison.

Introduction

The training systems of the twelve member states of the European Union have certain common, almost universal features:

1. women usually receive less training than men;
2. those with less education receive less training than those with more education;
3. those with less *initial* training receive less *continuing* training than those with more initial training;
4. the lower paid receive less training than the higher paid;
5. those who are employed in smaller firms normally receive less *formal* training than those employed in larger firms;
6. *most* of those who are employed in the private for-profit sector *usually* receive less training than those employed in the public sector;
7. younger employees usually receive more training than the oldest employees.

This list might be extended and refined once all the results are available from the European Union's Continuing Vocational Training Survey of 1994 and these can be matched to the data from the 1994 European Labour Force Survey. Nevertheless, reasonably robust generalizations of this kind can be made. It is far more difficult to move from statements about incidence, density and intensity of training to statements about learning outcomes, i.e. about the skills, knowledge, attitudes and values acquired as a result of training in different countries.

The reason for this is that a major dimension of reality is country-specific. In comparing qualified technicians in Germany, France and the United Kingdom (UK), Steedman and her colleagues (1991, Appendix I) reported on the balance which is struck in each country between general and specific knowledge within what are regarded across all three countries as broadly equivalent levels of practical competence and technical expertise. They found that the German qualification is likely to produce a quicker adaptation to workplace tasks and therefore a shorter period of initial adaptation training in company. The French and British qualifications included a mathematics content in excess of the needs of the science and physics in the curriculum. Moreover, the excess content was of a sort which is necessary to continue studies at degree level. In Germany, progression from technician-level to degree-level studies requires completion of a substantial bridging course as a condition of entry.

The different trade-offs in Germany, France and Britain between speedy acquisition of full workplace competence and laying a foundation for subsequent study reflect a difference in the priority given to competing objectives of competence and progression. Arguably, there is not always a single right way of deciding the content and objectives of training at a particular stage. A defensible case can be made for either the German or the Anglo-French choice.

For some purposes, qualified technicians in all three countries could be treated as comparably skilled. For other purposes, since competence goes beyond what is written in syllabuses and tested in written examinations, this would certainly not be the case. The reason for this is that the living social and economic context of training influences the nature, significance and value of outcomes. Without a grasp of the non-comparabilities which lie beneath apparent comparabilities, a simplistic interpretation of data on technical skills might easily lead to serious misunderstanding and ill-founded choices by employers and by governments. The fact that 'Britain produces proportionately as many technicians as France and considerably more than Germany' (op.cit.) may or may not be a matter of concern. That depends on the extent to which like is being compared with like in terms not merely of qualification, but in terms of the use and mix of skills at work, other factors making for productivity differentials, product mixes and the priorities of public policy.

It is necessary to turn to this context, and to the interaction between context and qualification, and to go beneath surface comparabilities. At this level, comparison of experience and data can be made productive even though the degree of comparability may be low.

The Benefits of Productive Comparison

The classic role of most cross-country comparisons is to help us to define and solve our own problems:

> Confrontation with a system built on assumptions somewhat different from our own brings those assumptions into relief. It causes us to question ideas which we might otherwise never question, and to think of alternatives we might never have thought of — of solutions, one might say, to problems we never realized we had. (Dore and Sako, 1989)

Here are a few assumptions which are challenged by comparative studies:

1   *That training is best provided by specialists in training*

> Maybe; but maybe not. Germany believes in specialist trainers, including the *Meister*, who are trained to train, but the Japanese speciality, on or off-the-job, is mutual teaching, and not by specialist trainers.

2   *That expenditure on off-the-job training, for example in France, is a good measure of the extent to which a firm is a committed learning organization*

> In Japan employees get a lot of informal, off-the-job training; and recognizable company training expenditures are scandalously low even by British standards. Off-the-job training is often provided through relatively cheap, low technology correspondence courses (which suit a rote learning, note-taking culture).
>
> The FORCE programme's 1994 in-company continuing training survey shows a strong predilection among German companies for workplace-based, low technology and uncertificated continuing training. Almost 60 per cent of firms did offer courses and seminars. But 82 per cent expressed a preference for other forms of continuing training, i.e. for information meetings (72 per cent), workplace-linked training (56 per cent) and self-guided learning (17 per cent). In workplace-linked training, coaching (41 per cent) and different forms of briefing (30–35 per cent) predominate, whereas quality circles (5 per cent) and job rotation (4 per cent) are not very common.

3   *That vocational qualifications tell us what their possessors have learned*

> To a significant, though variable degree, the qualifications of Japanese vocational high schools or the German dual system are the outcome of screening tests. They reflect the importance of the function of

training as a filter rather than a factory. The filter certifies useful personality characteristics, especially trainability.

It used to be claimed that the Opel plant in Cologne was the biggest bakery in Germany, because it employed so many *facharbeiter* who qualified in bakery. It did not employ all those bakers because their transferable skills in measuring quantities and mixing ingredients were useful in the paint shop. It employed them for two reasons:

   (i)   Because for years German bakeries produced four times as many *facharbeiter* as they could employ.

   (ii)   Because the *facharbeiterbrief* screens for willingness to work, to fit in and general learning ability.

4   *That definition, testing and certification of occupational standards is best left to employers, to self-regulating bodies of practitioners or to training institutions*

Both Japan and Germany are inclined to act on the assumption that only customers have an unalloyed interest in the maintenance of high standards. So they will not leave the job to these interested parties. The State must protect the customer interest.

What comparison offers is either an opportunity to challenge existing practice or to increase understanding of that practice.

Challenge: Less Maths Please, We're British

The National Institute of Economic and Social Research recently undertook a detailed comparison of construction workers with particular reference to the mathematical content of training (Steedman and Hawkins, 1994). The old (City and Guilds) training programme was comparable to the French CAP or the German Berufabschluss. Many of the mathematical elements formerly taught for City and Guilds are no longer specified or assessed in the National Vocational Qualification (NVQ) Level 2 replacement. These elements — and more besides — are required for building trade trainees of similar age and prior school attainments in France and Germany.

There are pluses, such as the certification of mature workers with experience but no diplomas, for which NVQs may be a suitable assessment instrument. But the NVQ in question is so occupationally specific and its content is so seriously weakened relative to its predecessor, that it cannot provide the broad preparation for working life which is nowadays required by young people. The investigators draw attention to additional negative factors such as the decline in the number of young people being certified, and the destabilizing effect of a form of financing whereby funding for training organizations is tied to the number of diplomas they grant. But the nub of the comparison concerns fitness for purpose.

Understanding: The Case of the Uncomplicated Biscuit

A recent investigation (Mason, van Ark and Wagner, 1994) compared productivity, machinery and skills in matched biscuit-making plants in the UK, Germany, the Netherlands and France. The study took account of inter-country differences in mix of product qualities. Quality-adjusted productivity levels were highest in Germany, 15 per cent above the Netherlands and France, 40 per cent above the UK. Differences in quality, measured by value-added per ton, were at least as great as differences in crude tonnage per person-hour. Big differences in workforce skill level seemed to link both to productivity performance and to each country's choice of product strategy. The mix of initial and continuing training in German plants supported a successful strategy in small and medium-batch production of elaborate, high value-added biscuits which others, especially the UK, would find if difficult to copy.

The greatest UK success was in large, very automated plants bulk-producing uncomplicated biscuits, i.e. a product with a rather low value-added. Even here, excessive rates of emergency down-time and the limitations of minimally and therefore very narrowly trained employees cost the British firms some of the potential economies of large scale production. The UK process workers had no vocational qualifications, roughly 40 per cent of those in the Netherlands and France qualified in junior vocational schools or to a higher level, and in Germany 90 per cent were bakery *facharbeiter*.

The investigators were able to control for equipment and quality differentials. There would be other factors, besides skill differentials, explaining the differences in productivity. For example, differences in the quality of management may have been a contributory factor. Usually it is a mosaic of interactive factors and conditions which explain cross-national variations in productivity. Nevertheless, the striking differences in the skills of process workers may be thought to prevent the British plants from competing at the high value-added end of the biscuit market. Whatever the problems of cross-national comparison of vocational qualifications, the differences at the level of process workers are too gross to admit of much uncertainty about the reason for the superior flexibility of the German relative to the British workforce.

Comparability Assessments

The difficulties begin when it is necessary to assess the degree of similarity between apparently similar training, assessments and qualifications. There are at least four key conditions which generally have to be met to establish a high level of comparability:

1   a common unit of measurement may be a necessary, but is never a sufficient basis for comparability of data between countries;

2   the object of measurement (e.g. training) and its context (all competence formation and the host economy and society) must be essentially similar;

3   only when input and process measures of training are complemented by data on content and outcomes can comparability be evaluated;

4   outcomes from training cannot be assessed for comparability unless they include not only the more immediate outcomes such as trainee reactions, skill mastery and job competence, but also the remote effects such as changed attitudes, organizational change, and effects on competitiveness and profitability.

However well training is measured by volume, expenditure or outcome, there is no certain foundation for causal hypotheses in any cross-section correlation between training effort and competitive performance. The nexus of causes which promote economic performance are rarely the same from country to country, any more than they are within the same country at different periods in its history or between industry sectors at the same moment in time. Benchmarking against the training given by admired competitors, whether countries or companies, can result in a naïve kind of causality hypothesis.

Generally there are many intervening variables which are far more powerful than training. The workforce qualification profiles of Belarus and of Britain are virtually identical at all the principal levels, i.e. primary and secondary schooling and higher education. But even before the collapse of the Soviet Union, real gross domestic product per head in Belarus was only half that in Britain, and it is now approaching one third. Explanatory variables other than education and training must be more important.

On the other hand, benchmarking of the type exemplified by National Institute studies is able to pose questions with a precision which is not otherwise attainable. When that precision is attained it is equally essential to come to a judgment on the degree to which comparability matters and how far the four conditions outlined above are met.

It is worth listing the constraints on comparability, some or all of which are present in every cross-national comparison:

(i)   it is impossible to characterize statistically the work-led competence formation (on-the-job learning) which complements and can sometimes be a substitute for instruction-led competence formation. National skills certification tests do not always recognize important job-specific skills, nor do test scores correlate with some of the most important ingredients of firm productivity, i.e. with 'team skills' and 'work habits' (see Timmerman, 1993; Levin and Kelley, 1994). The ability of exams to measure skills valued by employers is often exaggerated;

(ii)   training is a necessary but not a sufficient condition of economic growth or company competitiveness (see Timmerman, 1993; Levin and Kelly, 1994).

(iii)   the remoter effects of training on organizations are even more difficult to attribute to preceding training than the more immediate effects;

(iv)   social effects of training, such as value change, the social re-integration of the un-employed and the consequences of these for families and local communities are as difficult to measure as they are to attribute confidently to training;

(v)   some effects make themselves felt only over long periods of time and are cumulative. High training firms grow more than average and do even more training. The more initial training individuals receive, the more continuing training they get. The families of the most highly trained members of the workforce are better-off than the average family and are more likely to produce highly educated and trained children;

(vi)   analytical separation of investment in skills and knowledge from investment in physical capital is very common. It completely obscures the essentially complementary nature of much human and physical capital formation;

(vii)   data aggregation quickly destroys information on the objectives and content of training, without which it is not possible to understand its social and economic role and to evaluate its comparability with training in other countries.

Comparison with Low Comparability

In making productive comparisons, it is as important to assess for difference as for similarity, both between the activities being assessed and their contexts. Devising sensible evaluative frameworks and techniques for defining challenging comparators are crucial to productive comparison.

There are certain basic axioms:

1   training is only one kind of competence formation;
2   work organization is pivotal in the demand for, the production and the use of competencies;
3   knowledge of workplace realities is essential to any understanding of the big picture of a national training system.

It is essential to control for differences in the inner and outer environments of training. Although it is not possible to do this statistically, except in a partial and descriptive fashion, it is important to do it explicitly, otherwise the process of judgment formation is unchallengeable. All that is visible is the net result.

The inner or immediate environment of competence formation (Figure 5.1) powerfully influences the value attached to qualifications and therefore the motivation of individuals to invest. In a country like the United States, where the corporate response to intensified competition on the global market

---

The Inner Environment

- the way work is organized

- the way people are recruited, paid and promoted

- employer systems for developing people (HRD programmes, career structures, the architecture of internal labour markets)

Figure 5.1: The inner environment

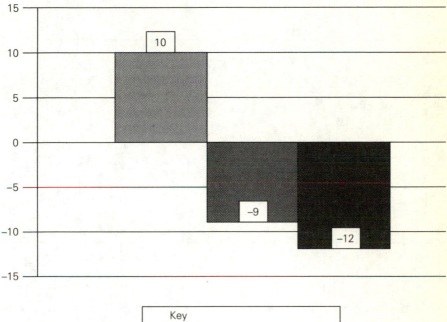

Key

Male college graduates

High school graduates

High school dropouts

Figure 5.2: Percentage change in US real incomes in the 1980s

can be, and is, to out source production to Asia or Latin America or to cut the real wages of those workers in direct competition with Asian and Latin American workers, it is possible to have a complete reversal of the labour market value of less-educated and less-skilled workers (Figure 5.2).

In continental Europe, the burden of a similar requirement to adjust cost

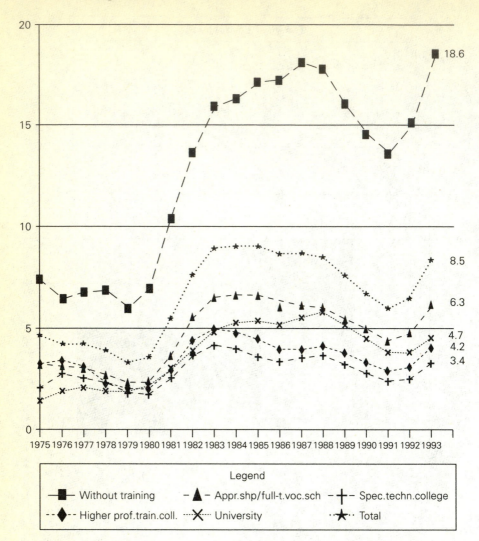

* Unemployed as a percentage of dependently employed persons (excluding apprentices and soldiers) with the same qualifications; 1990–93 preliminary estimates. (Buttler and Tessaring, 1994)

Figure 5.3: Qualification-related unemployment rates (in per cent) West Germany 1975–93*

structures generally took the form of steeper rises in unemployment among the unskilled or semi-skilled. In Germany, the share of earnings of those without completed training fell sharply from 1976 to 1991, the earnings share of those with completed apprenticeships or vocational school training rose until 1980 but then flattened out for the rest of the decade, and the earnings share of all the more highly qualified rose sharply (Buttler and Tessaring, 1994, p. 8). As Figure 5.3 shows, in an occupational labour market such as that in

	The Outer Environment
	• the structuring of primary and secondary labour markets
	• available technologies
	• product markets
	• law on taxation of companies and individuals
	• relationships between the initial education system, labour markets and firms

Figure 5.4: The outer environment

	Profits retained for re-investment as per cent of total profits, 1975–92	**Average annual rate of economic growth, 1960–80**	**Value added per worker, $ 1985**
Germany	67	3.7	–
Japan	63	7.7	31,000
USA	54	3.5	46,000
France	54	4.6	–
Britain	45	2.3	24,000

Sources: Datastream; *Economist* 24.10.92

Figure 5.5: Profit re-investment 1975–92

Germany, the risk of unemployment is very systematically ordered according to qualification level, whatever the stage of the business cycle.

That the influence of the outer environment (Figure 5.4) on the value attached to training and to qualifications is less direct but no less important is easily illustrated:

(i)   Managerial Short-termism

The data on profit re-investment (Figure 5.5) show that British firms do not re-invest as enthusiastically as firms in competitor countries. In Germany, much of industry is controlled by private, unquoted companies. Even the small number of publicly-quoted companies have a share-owning structure in which bank holdings and cross-holdings by suppliers and customers constitute, in effect, long-term capital. By contrast, three-quarters of Britain's gross national product comes from publicly-quoted companies and there is a very liquid capital market.

Firms operating under German company law and finance are able to pursue market share and long-term competitive pricing much more easily than British firms. Other factors also help to explain the very different investment behaviour of British and German firms. But one factor contributing to the shortness of managerial time horizons in Britain is its company law and liquid capital market, together with the remuneration systems for managers. It is unsurprising if the general investment characteristics of British and German firms spill over into their attitude to human capital formation. One country's firms tend to favour just-in-time job training; the other long-term, strategic and occupational training.

(ii)   *The Role of Legislation*

In Germany there is a regulated continuing training market operating alongside a larger, firm-driven unregulated and uncertificated one. The role of legislation is considerable in Germany, as it is in France, and in both cases far more so than it is in Italy or Britain. However, there is a big difference between German and French legislation, especially in continuing training. French legislation concentrates heavily on the training role of the employer. In Germany, federal intervention via the law is directed at individuals: it gives them legal or financial rights or protection as consumers. Acts and regulations are not aimed as a rule at employers or at training institutions.

To make sense of these very different forms of intervention it is necessary to look at the whole outer environment, plus the inner environment. It is the net effect, the interaction of many contextual features which counts. In comparing Japan and Germany to Britain, Sako (1990) pointed out that both of the well-functioning systems had established a high skills equilibrium, with a broad-based school curriculum, high staying-on rates in full- or part- time post-16 education and training, strong inter-firm relations (i.e. the Chambers and the Keiretsu) and a corporatist structure to legitimize policy decisions. Until very recently the narrower British curriculum had a noticeable anti-industrial bias, a large dispersion in attainments and lower staying-on rates. Co-operative inter-firm relations are notoriously weak or non-existent in Britain, which relies heavily on deregulated markets. The State role has been inconsistent, shifting backwards and forwards between *laissez-faire* and regulation.

Yet apprenticeship training, so fundamental to initial training in Germany, is not fundamental in Japan, and labour markets which are external and occupational in Germany are more internal in Japan. Vocational qualifications are crucial to pay determination in Germany; in Japan, vocational qualifications matter less and seniority and merit more. It is not any single dimension of the environment but the complex integration of enterprise training within a far wider and unique context which determines the effectiveness of a total system in mobilizing human potential.

Conclusion

No skill or knowledge test will successfully rank a worker in all firms in an economy: how much less in economies other than that in which that worker's competencies were formed? This is not to argue against standardized testing and certification of easily-measured knowledge and skills; nor against cross-national comparisons of what is similar and what is different. Such comparisons act as a reminder that certain important skills are inherently hard-to-measure; and that the role and value of some clusters of skills may be specific to a particular country, just as some skills have little or no value outside a particular firm or industry.

More positively, in the usual case — where comparability between countries is low — comparison can still yield useful returns by challenging assumptions or promoting a better understanding both of problems and of the lines along which solutions might be sought.

References

BUTTLER, F. and TESSARING, M. (1994) *Human Capital as a Location Factor: Arguments for the Education Policy Discussion From a Labour Market Policy Standpoint*, IAB Labour Market Research Topic 8, Nürnburg, Institut für Arbeitsmarkt-und Berufsforschung.

DORE, R.P. and SAKO, M. (1989) *How the Japanese Learn to Work*, London, Routledge.

LEVIN, H.M. and KELLEY, C. (1994) 'Can education do it alone?', *Economics of Education Review*, **13**, 2, June.

MASON, G., VAN ARK, B. and WAGNER, K. (1994) 'Productivity, product quality and workforce skills: Food processing in four european countries', *National Institute Economic Review*, **147**, February.

SAKO, M. (1990) 'Enterprise training in a comparative perspective: West Germany, Japan and Britain', unpublished report for the World Bank, London, London School of Economics.

STEEDMAN, H. and HAWKINS, J. (1994) 'Shifting foundations: The impact of NVQs on youth training for the building trades', *National Institute Economic Review*, **149**, August.

STEEDMAN, H., MASON, G. and WAGNER, K. (1991) 'Intermediate skills in the workplace: Deployment, standards and supply in Britain, France and Germany', *National Institute Economic Review*, **136**, May.

TIMMERMAN, D. (1993) 'Costs and financing of the dual system in Germany: Is there any lesson for other countries?', unpublished paper for International Symposium on the Economics of Education, Manchester, UK, May.

National Issues

6   Comparing the Standards of Examining Groups in the United Kingdom

Ben Jones and Peter Ratcliffe

Summary

It is important to distinguish between two distinct meanings to which the term 'standard' is put in the context of public examinations. Either the term can apply to the general level of attainment of a cohort/group of students (e.g. 'the standard of students' English is not what it was ten years ago'), or it can apply to the criteria for performance demanded by examiners at specific grades in an examination (e.g. 'English is easier than mathematics'). It is with the latter definition that this chapter is concerned. The second part of the chapter provides a brief outline of how a comparability geography study was organized, an overview of its findings and raises a number of issues for further consideration.

Introduction

Figure 6.1 contains three of the main types of comparability which are the province of research into standards and it is the third of these, comparability within the same subject between different examining groups, that is the particular focus of this chapter.

Comparability of examination standards	• between year (same syllabuses) • between subjects (same examination group) • between groups (same subjects)

Figure 6.1:   Types of comparability

Confidence about inter-group comparability of standards is important for several reasons. It ensures that:

(i)   individuals with the same level of achievement have equal access to opportunities of employment and further education;

(ii)   schools, which are increasingly judged by their students' results in public examinations, are compared according to a common yardstick;

(iii) society operates efficiently; a meritocratic system will be inhibited if the same grades reflect different levels of achievement with different groups.

In recent years the government has also indicated its commitment to inter-group comparability by appointing external assessors whose task it is to ensure that standards between General Certificate of Secondary Education (GCSE) groups are maintained.

Background

The GCSE is a subject specific examination taken by most students in the United Kingdom (UK) at the end of their compulsory education at age 16.

Virtually all students take examinations in core subjects, English, mathematics and science, but the average number of subjects taken is eight. GCSE grades are, therefore, the currency with which students purchase opportunities in employment and represent the only hard currency they have by way of qualifications when applying for, and being offered places at, university. Offers will be made primarily on the basis of performance at GCSE and those grades are, therefore, very important.

The GCSE examination is administered by four examining groups in England plus one each in Wales and Northern Ireland. It is graded on a seven grade scale, A–G with U = unclassified/fail. Figure 6.2 depicts the overall grade distribution for 1993.

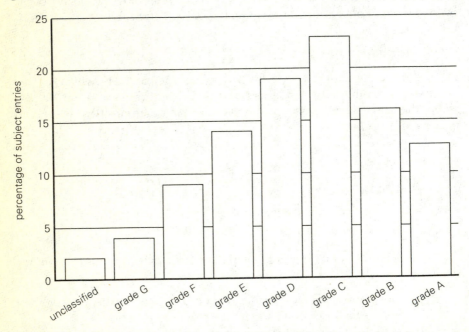

Figure 6.2: Combined GCSE results for the six GCSE Examining Groups in the United Kingdom, 1993

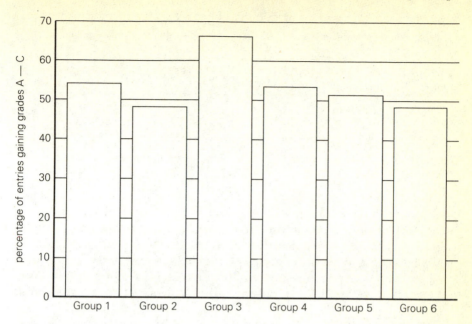

Figure 6.3:   Percentage of geography entries awarded grades A–C for each of the six GCSE Groups, 1993

The location of the A, C, F grade boundaries on the mark distribution is decided judgmentally by senior examiners, based on the quality of candidates' work. These grades are, therefore, critical as they represent the benchmark of standards. The other grade boundaries are determined arithmetically, either by interpolation or extrapolation.

Statistics

Figure 6.3 depicts the percentage of each Group's candidates gaining grades A–C in geography in 1993. Clearly it cannot be concluded from this graph that the standard demanded of Group 3's examination is lenient and that of Group 2's severe — there are far too many factors which could explain these differences apart from the relative severity/leniency of the examiners in the different groups. Some of these factors are listed in Figure 6.4.

Although it is only (a) and (b) which should be controlled for when comparing examinations statistics, (c) will tend to affect these, and so in controlling for them, one will unwittingly control for (c) also.

The existence of this problem is one of the main reasons why the cross-moderation technique is currently the most favoured way of making inter-group comparisons. Before considering the methodology of this technique, however, it is worth reporting how the GCSE groups attempt to control, albeit

(a) individual effects	(ability; prior achievement; motivation; gender; socio-economic background)
(b) school effects	(grouped individual effects; entry policy; teacher effectiveness)
(c) examination paper and syllabus effects	

Figure 6.4:   Possible factors explaining differences in Groups' raw grade distributions

in a crude manner, for student/centre effects. For each candidate, groups routinely collect the type of centre through which his/her examination entries are made. With respect to performance, these centre types are known to be relatively homogeneous — students in independent and selective schools, for example, tending to get better results. (It should be noted, however, that most variation still exists within centre type.) The profile of a group's grade distribution will, therefore, tend to depend on the balance of centre types in its entry.

The relationship between percentage of candidates gaining grades A–C and the percentage of candidates from independent or selective centres can be expanded by controlling for all centre types simultaneously. The method for doing this has been called the Delta Index, and the resultant, adjusted values give a better, though by no means definitive, indication of groups' relative severity/leniency than the raw figures. Details of the Delta Index as it was applied to different geography syllabuses in 1993 are given in the **statistical review (1993 examination statistics)** section of this chapter.

Cross-moderation Studies at GCSE

Even if student and school level factors could be statistically controlled for more efficiency, a lot of assumptions would still need to be made about students, centres and, perhaps most pertinently factors relating to different groups' examination/syllabuses. There have been several attempts to make statistical comparisons between groups by using measures of individual student's prior attainment, ability and motivation as the control variables. These studies have, necessarily, been on a smaller scale and despite having better quality data at individual level, definitive answers about observed inter-group differences inevitably remain elusive due to the inability to control for all the necessary factors, especially those which are examination/syllabus related. The work of the A-level Information System (ALIS), based at the University of Newcastle upon Tyne, which compares GCE A-level Boards, comes into this category. Despite its expense it has, therefore, been recognized that the cross-moderation approach, which requires senior examiners to compare the work of candidates deemed to be of an equivalent standard, is the most appropriate way of making inter-group comparisons.

In both 1988 (the first year of the GCSE examination) and 1989 the GCSE Groups undertook cross-moderation studies in five subjects. These were ratification studies in which experienced, senior examiners considered the work of a sample of students at the three judgmental boundary marks: A, C, F from each group. They were required to rate the work of each student according to where they believed it to be in relation to the relevant grade boundary.

In 1992, the Groups embarked on another series of studies in the core subjects, English, mathematics and science, and used the exercise to incorporate three experimental changes to the design in an attempt to improve the reliability of the results achieved. These three design features were as follows:

1 independent subject experts, as opposed to 'in-house' GCSE senior examiners, were used as scrutineers to make the judgments. The design particularly tried to avoid the situation where one group's examiners judged other groups' standards in terms of the knowledge and skills required by their own group, with the result that other groups were likely to be deemed to be more lenient than their own. This design feature made the introduction of the second main difference of design, described in (2) below, even more important;

2 the scrutineers were asked to make their judgments with reference to certain objective factors, for example 'content' and 'context', since, unlike examiners used in previous studies, they did not have an internalized standard of what was expected at grades A and C;

3 the scrutineers were asked to evaluate the relative demands of the question papers, mark schemes and syllabuses before looking at candidates' work.

Due to the inordinate amount of time taken by the independent subject experts to review the scripts, design feature (1) was dropped for the 1993 GCSE Comparability Studies in geography and history. Features (2) and (3) were, however, retained, and the following sections describe the methodology and results of the geography study.

A Comparability Study in GCSE Geography Based on the Summer 1993 Examinations

For this study one main syllabus from each of the six examining groups in the UK was used. Each group provided the complete work of a sample of candidates at each of the three key grade boundaries A/B, C/D and F/G. In addition each Examining Group nominated three senior examiners to act as scrutineers in the study. The design of the 1993 geography study consisted of three strands: a statistical analysis, a syllabus review and a cross-moderation study. Each strand is described briefly below and examined in more detail later in the paper.

The statistical review involved an analysis of both the raw results of the six syllabuses in the study and the adjusted results which had made an allowance for the different candidatures attracted by each group.

The syllabus review consisted of an analysis by the scrutineers of the demands made by each of the syllabuses in the study. Each of the syllabuses (including the associated question papers and mark schemes) was rated in relation to four factors: content; skills and processes; structure and manageability; and practical skills. This review was completed prior to a residential cross-moderation study.

The cross-moderation study took the form of a ratification study in which the scrutineers gave ratings for each set of work from each group, except their own. The ratings given by the scrutineers indicated whether the work was judged to be better than borderline (+), worse than borderline (−) or typical of the boundary region (0).

Statistical Review (1993 Examination Statistics)

The six syllabuses reviewed accounted for 45.7 per cent of the national entry of the Mode 1 Geography syllabuses in 1993. The review considered both the raw results and the adjusted results, i.e. once allowance had been made for the different candidatures attracted by each group. The raw results suggested potential differences between the groups in particular at grades A to C. For example, Group 4 awarded 18.7 per cent of its candidates grade A, whilst Group 5 awarded grade A to only 10 per cent of its candidates. At grade C the cumulative percentage of candidates achieving grade C and above ranged from 47.8 per cent to 65.7 per cent. Nevertheless, these differences need to be considered in relation to the different candidatures attracted to each syllabus. For example, Groups 1 and 4 had over a quarter of their entry from independent schools whilst only 3.6 per cent of the entry for Group 6 came from such schools. In contrast 96.8 per cent of the entry for Group 3 came from LEA maintained selective or secondary modern schools with no candidates from comprehensive, grant maintained, sixth form or tertiary colleges.

In order to make allowance for such differences a technique known as the Delta Index which takes account of the proportions of candidates from each type of centre was used. In essence the Delta Index compares the relative percentages of candidates achieving a grade within a centre type. The difference between a group's distribution and the total distribution within each centre type (weighted by the number of candidates relative to a group's total

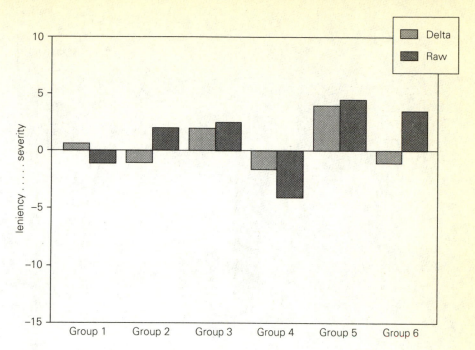

Figure 6.5:   Grade A

entry) is then aggregated to provide the Delta Index. The entry was divided into eleven centre categories used by all the examining groups and those categories have been included in the Delta Index calculations provided in the figures below. Two of the centre type categories were Secondary Comprehensive Schools (LEA and Grant Maintained). It is acknowledged that the comprehensive centre type covers a wide range of attainment, and therefore that some groups may attract 'better' comprehensives than others. In order to allow for this wide range of schools, each comprehensive centre was allocated to one of six equal categories based on the examination performance of the schools. Consequently the Delta Index was based on fifteen centre types with male and female results available separately for each centre type. The following Figures 6.5, 6.6 and 6.7 show both the raw results and the adjusted (Delta) results. The vertical axes of the figures give the difference between the expected cumulative percentage of candidates and the actual cumulative percentage of candidates attaining grades A, C and F. Figure 6.5 suggests that, although Group 4 awarded the highest proportion of grade As, when allowance is made of the types of centre, it is in line with the other Groups. At the other end of the scale Group 5 awarded the lowest proportion of grade As, with only a slight change to its position when the Delta Index is applied. The findings for Group 6 are interesting in that the raw data indicated a degree of

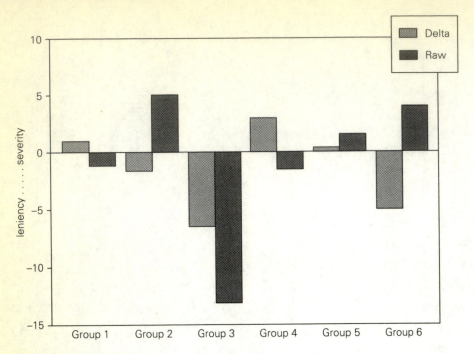

Figure 6.6:   Grades A–C

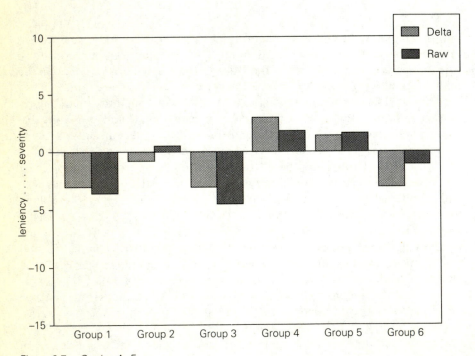

Figure 6.7:   Grades A–F

severity yet when the Delta Index was applied the Group appeared to be relatively lenient. Similarly from Figure 6.6, the raw data indicate that Group 2 awarded the lowest proportion of grades A–C, although when allowance is made for the types of centre, it is seen to be in line with the other Groups. Again for Group 3 the raw data suggest that Group 3 awarded the highest proportion of grades A–C, yet when centre type is included in the analysis the perceived leniency is dramatically reduced. Group 3 is in a part of the UK where the vast majority of centres are maintained grammar schools or secondary modern schools, which could account to some extent for the different pattern of awards. The findings for Group 6 are interesting in that the raw data included a degree of severity yet when the Delta Index was applied Group 6 appeared to be relatively lenient. As may be noted from Figure 6.7 the differences between the groups in the cumulative percentages of candidates, for grade F and above, are much less for both the raw and adjusted percentages. Group 4, which awarded the highest proportion of grade As, awarded the lowest proportion of grades at grade F and above, with the application of the Delta Index actually increasing the difference.

Syllabus Review

The syllabus review involved a comparison of the relative demands of the total examination package (syllabus, question papers and mark schemes) in relation to the four factors: content; skills and processes; structure and manageability and practical skills. The review of the content was carried out in relation to the requirements and demands of the syllabus and its associated question papers. Skills and processes were rated in terms of understanding, application and values whilst structure and manageability was viewed in the more specific aspects of question difficulty, language, layout and context. Practical skills were rated particularly in relation to field work skills necessary for the Geographical Enquiry but also in terms of those practical skills examined on the question papers. The factors had been developed from discussion of earlier work by Pollitt *et al.* (1985).

The purpose of the review was to determine whether or not some of the syllabuses, question papers and mark schemes were perceived as more demanding or less demanding than others. Nevertheless, it should be borne in mind that a relatively difficult syllabus and examination might be compensated for at the awarding stage and therefore be comparable with a less demanding syllabus and examination where the awarding required relatively high marks to be attained at each boundary. Each of the eighteen scrutineers involved in the study were asked to provide a rating for each group's syllabus (including the coursework requirements), examination papers and mark schemes on each of the four factors. The ratings were given on a scale of 1 to 5 (undemanding to very demanding). The scrutineers also provided comments qualifying their decisions, particularly at ratings of 1 or 5.

Cross-moderation Study

As may be noted from Figure 6.8 there was considerable agreement between the scrutineers in the cross-moderation study about the comparability of standards at grade A of Groups 1, 2, 3, 4 and 5. Group 6 was seen as the most lenient group at this boundary. None of the ratings for this group were +, and 64.6 per cent were – ratings. A comparison of pairs of the groups' ratings using the Scheffé multiple comparison test,[1] provided four sets of statistically significant differences between Group 6 and Groups 1, 2, 3, and 5. At grade C (see Figure 6.9) there were nine categories because three of the groups had two distinct routes to grade C. Six of the nine routes were given similar ratings by the scrutineers. There was general agreement about the relative leniency of Group 3 (lower route) and Group 6 (both routes). When considering each of the differentiated routes to grade C, it is interesting to note that the 'harder' route was judged to be relatively severe compared with the 'easier' route. This finding corroborates the findings of Good and Cresswell (1988), that is, that awarders generally judged fewer candidates to have reached the required standard for a grade when the component was harder. There was substantial agreement with the original grading at this boundary (see Figure 6.10). There was also general agreement (as at A and C) about the leniency of Group 6. A comparison of pairs of the Groups' ratings using the Scheffé test indicated three sets of statistically significant differences between Group 6 and each of Groups 2, 3, and 4.

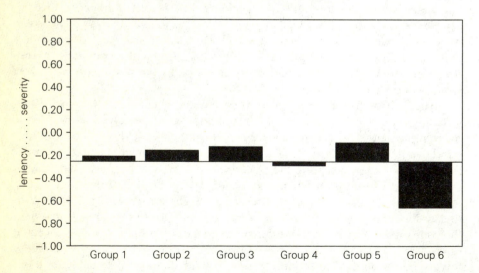

Figure 6.8: Mean ratings of scrutineers A/B boundary by syllabus

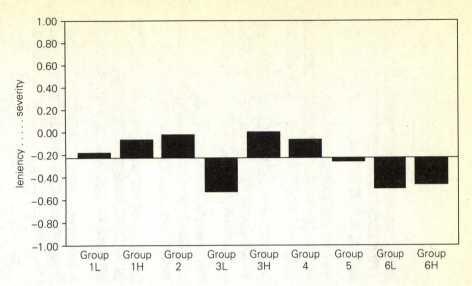

Figure 6.9:   *Mean rating of scrutineers C/D boundary by syllabus*

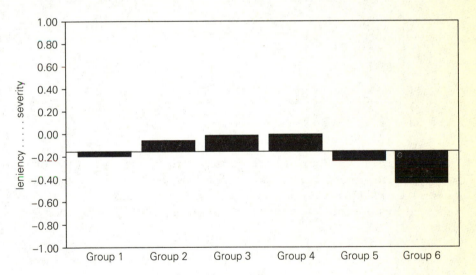

Figure 6.10:   *Mean ratings of scrutineers F/G boundary by syllabus*

Scrutineer Performances

Given the broadly similar ratings for each group, with the exception of Group 6, it might have been expected that the patterns of ratings for each group's scrutineers would also be similar. In the case of Group 6 scrutineers, it could be expected that given that they were rated as generous in their awards, they would see the awarding of the other groups as relatively severe.

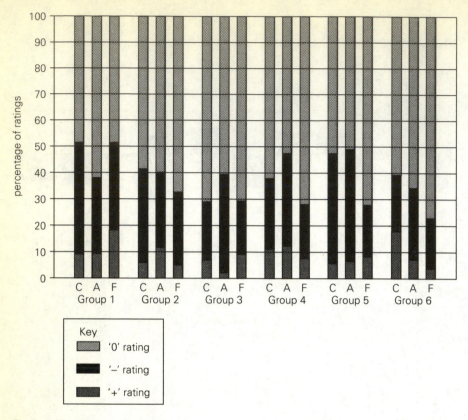

Figure 6.11: Ratings of scrutineers' groups

However, these expectations were only partially met in that the differences between groups' scrutineers were relatively small and the group 6 scrutineers were also generous in their ratings, except at grade C. A number of other patterns of ratings by scrutineers' groups may also be recognized from Figure 6.11.

The Group 5 scrutineers produced a different pattern of ratings at grade F compared with grades A and C. Similarly Group 3 scrutineers produced a different pattern of ratings at A compared with grades C and F.

Consistency of the Ratings

Here the analysis assumed that each of the eighteen scrutineers made consistent judgments throughout the exercise on each set of work reviewed. The design of the study ensured that each set of work would be reviewed by a number of scrutineers and that there would be work in common to the scrutineers from the same group. This allowed an analysis of the level of agreement between scrutineers on the common sets of work by means of pairings of scrutineers. An analysis of the rating agreements of the scrutineers using pairings of common candidates gave an overall inter-scrutineer consistency of 54.2 per cent. The largest level of inter-scrutineer agreement was found at the F/G boundary. Nevertheless, it should be recognized that a high proportion of agreements does not necessarily imply that the scrutineers thought standards were comparable between groups. It could be argued that if scrutineers believed that standards were definitely not comparable, in some cases, this might be reflected in a high number of agreements that some groups were out of line and, conversely in a situation where standards were broadly comparable, it might be expected that there would be a large number of disagreements since the difference in standards between candidates' work would be marginal. An analysis was made of the way in which the three scrutineers from each examining group rated the other groups. At all three grade boundaries each group's scrutineers (with the exception of one group at grade F) did not rate the other examining groups as severe in comparison with their own group. The tendency of examiners to judge their own group's standards to be more severe than the other groups is a common feature of comparability studies (Forrest and Shoesmith, 1985). As in previous studies the scrutineers rated the other groups more lenient than their own. Even the scrutineers from the group which was rated the most lenient had this view of the other groups' work.

Conclusion

In order to evaluate the comparability of the six geography syllabuses used in the study this section of the chapter has brought together the following evidence: the findings from the cross-moderation study; the examination statistics for 1993 (raw and Delta Indices); the findings from the syllabus review, and the qualitative commentaries provided by the scrutineers on the syllabus review, cross-moderation and on the application of the assessment of spelling, punctuation and grammar.

The syllabus review found little variation in the ratings between syllabuses. Nevertheless, in relation to three of these factors (content, skills and processes and structure and manageability), Group 2 was seen as relatively less demanding while Group 3 was relatively more demanding. Group 6 was considered to have an average level of demand for all four factors.

The results of the cross-moderation study indicated that there was a general agreement from the cross-moderation study about the comparability of standards. However, the perceived leniency of Group 6 at each of the three boundaries was recognized.

The results from the statistical analyses show that when allowance for differences in centre types is made, the grade distributions of the groups converge. The exception was that the apparent severity as shown by the raw data of Group 6 at grades A and C, became leniency with the application of the Delta Index.

Note

1   The Scheffé method is conservative for pairwise comparisons of means. It requires larger differences between means for significance than most other multiple comparison tests.

References

FITZ-GIBBON, C.T., TYMMS, P.B. and VINCENT, L. (1994) *Comparing Examination Boards and Syllabuses at A-level: Students' Grades, Attitudes and Perceptions of Classroom Processes: Executive Summary*, A-level Information System, Curriculum, Evaluation and Management Centre, University of Newcastle upon Tyne.

FORREST, G.M. and SHOESMITH, D.J. (1985) *A Second Review of GCE Comparability Studies*, Manchester, Joint Matriculation Board on behalf of the GCE Examining Boards.

GOOD, F. and CRESSWELL, M. (1988) *Grading the GCSE*, London, Secondary Examinations Council.

NORTHERN EXAMINATIONS AND ASSESSMENT BOARD/INTER-GROUP RESEARCH COMMITTEE (1994) *A Comparability Study in GCSE Geography: A Study Based on the Summer 1993 Examinations*, Northern Examinations and Assessment Board on behalf of the Inter-Group Research Committee for the GCSE.

POLLITT, A., HUTCHINSON, C., ENTWISTLE, N. and DE LUCA, C. (1985) *What Makes Exam Questions Difficult?*, Edinburgh, Scottish Academic Press.

STOBART, G. (1990) *GCSE Inter-Group Comparability Study, 1989: Geography*, London, London and East Anglian Group on behalf of the Inter-Group Research Committee.

TYMMS, P.B. and VINCENT, L. (1994) *Comparing Examination Boards and Syllabuses at A-level: Students' Grade, Attitudes and Perceptions of Classroom Processes: Technical Report*, A-level Information System, Curriculum, Evaluation and Management Centre, University of Newcastle upon Tyne.

7 Standard-setting Methods for Multiple Levels of Competence

Dylan Wiliam

Summary

Although the National Curriculum of England and Wales has undergone several revisions since its inception in 1988, the main features of its assessment have remained largely unchanged. Namely:

- all pupils are assessed at the ages of 7, 11, 14 and 16 (the end of each of the four 'key stages' of education);
- the assessments are to be criterion-referenced;
- the results are based on both teachers' judgments and the results of external tests;
- the assessments of pupils [apart from those at 16] are reported on a scale of age-independent levels (Secretary of State for Education and Science, 1988).

During the development of National Curriculum assessment in England, Wales and Northern Ireland, a variety of innovative scoring models for the external tests were piloted. Many of these were inconsistent with 'good practice' in aggregation (Cresswell, 1994) and so, from 1994 on, the level achieved on the test is to be determined entirely by unweighted summation of marks and the teachers' judgments and the test levels are to be reported separately.

This decision returned National Curriculum assessment to the 'mainstream' of educational and psychological measurement, but has also raised some new challenges. The problem of setting cut-scores for minimum competency tests is well-addressed in the literature, but there is very little about how multiple cut-scores can be set for different levels of competence, as required in National Curriculum assessment.

This chapter discusses some of the standard-setting methods that have been proposed for multiple levels of competence and describes and evaluates the results of some recent attempts at standard-setting for National Curriculum tests in mathematics and science.

Introduction

The term 'standard' is used in a variety of ways. Hambleton (1978) gives this example:

> School district A has set the following target. It desires to have 85 per cent or more of its students in the second grade achieve 90 per cent of the reading objectives at a standard of performance equal to or better than 80 per cent.

There are three kinds of standards involved in this example, relating to the proportion of:

1   items relating to a particular objective answered correctly by an individual student (80 per cent);
2   objectives to be achieved by each student (90 per cent);
3   students reaching the specified achievements (85 per cent).

Standard-setting in National Curriculum assessment involves aspects of all three of these kinds of standards.

Allocating a student to one of the levels of the eight-level scale can be viewed as a series of dichotomous classifications — i.e. has the candidate reached level 4 or not? level 5? level 6? If achievement is measured simply by the total number of items answered correctly (so that any two candidates with the same total score are regarded as equivalent — essentially a 'Rasch' model) then standard-setting involves no more that setting a cut-score, and assigning mastery status to those that reach the cut-score, and non-mastery status to those who do not.

Although it may be possible to identify items in the National Curriculum tests with a particular level, since all correct answers are weighted equally, the levels serve primarily to stratify the domain from which the individual items are drawn. This means that the first and second kinds of standards are not distinguished in National Curriculum assessment.

The third kind of standard enters into the setting of the cut-score because of the design considerations involved in the ten-level scale. The original motivation for the ten-level scale required that, initially at least, most of the levels should be calibrated in terms of the median attainment of different age-cohorts (median 10-year-olds should be minimally competent at level 4, median 12-year-olds at level 5 and so on). While this will become less and less important as the standards 'float-free' of their original norm-referenced beginnings, paying attention to the third kind of standard ensures that distributions of scores are not too much at variance with public expectations.

The foregoing has discussed standards only in terms of particular fixed points. Wanting 85 per cent of students to achieve 90 per cent of a domain will place special emphasis around these particularly emphasized regions. It says nothing about what proportion of the students would achieve 50 per cent of the objectives. Standards are usually discussed in unidimensional terms, even though the concept of standard involves a *distribution* of attainment through-out the population, and the shape of the distribution, apart from at the one point specified by the standard, is often ignored. So for example, the same *reported* 'standard' could mask quite different distributions of attainment, and this is particularly important when comparing populations from different countries or cultural groups. There is evidence, for example, that the 'tolerance of variability' — i.e. the extent to which a wide range of performance levels in a particular age cohort is acceptable — is much greater in the United Kingdom (UK) than, for example in the United States (US) and Japan (Robitaille and Garden, 1988; Schaub and Baker, 1991).

Standard-setting Procedures

In his 'consumer's guide' to standard-setting methods, Berk (1986) identifies thirty-eight different procedures, twenty-three of which are methods for setting standards and fifteen of which are procedures for adjusting them in the light of empirical data about their consequences. He classified the methods according to the degree to which empirical evidence about the effects of a particular choice of cut-score is fed into the procedure. In the past, methods have been described as either *judgmental* or *empirical*, but such a classification is unhelpful since all standard-setting procedures involve judgment, are essentially arbitrary (Hambleton, 1980), and cannot be discussed independently of a system of values (Messick, 1989). For this reason, in this paper, I will refer to *test-centred* methods, *examinee-centred* methods, and *combination* methods (Jaeger, 1989):

test-centred methods	no empirical evidence is used in determining the cut-score
combination methods	empirical data is used to complement or refine the choice of cut-score
examinee-centred methods	the choice of cut-score is based primarily on the distribution of scores, although judgmental factors feed into the definitions of, for example, 'minimum competency'.

Eleven of the twenty-three standard-setting methods described by Berk are 'test-centred', seven are 'combination methods', and five are 'examinee-centred'.

Cutting across this continuum from examinee-centred to test-centred methods is another which relates to the extent to which the standard-setting procedure is completed before the test is developed or implemented. For example, many assessments are *designed* to have cut-scores in the region of 50 per cent because a public expectation has been built up that suggests that this is where the 'pass-mark' will be. Other, 'mastery-oriented' assessments might be designed to have cut-scores set at higher marks (say 70 per cent or 80 per cent), but the important idea is that the tests are designed with a particular cut-score in mind. For other tests, the primary requirement might be to ensure representative sampling from a domain, so that where the 'best' cut-score might be found is a secondary consideration. Put crudely, is the cut-score adjusted to fit the items, or are the items adjusted to fit the cut-score? Of course, these are not discrete approaches but opposite ends of a continuum; approaches involving pre-determining a cut-score might be described as *policy-oriented methods* and those that adjust the cut-scores in the light of the actual composition of the test, or the performance of candidates as *data-oriented methods*. These two dimensions (centering: examinee v test and orientation: policy v data) if treated dichotomously, give rise to four categories of standard-setting methods, which are discussed in turn below.

Policy-oriented Test-centred Procedures

In 1984, Sir Keith Joseph called for the results of school-leaving examinations in England and Wales to give far greater information about what a candidate could actually do (Secretary of State for Education and Science, 1984). What-ever his original intentions, the demand was interpreted as a requirement for the grades awarded in school-leaving examinations to provide detailed informa-tion about the skills and competencies it was reasonable to expect a candidate with a particular grade to have demonstrated in the examination. The difficulty was that the unreliability of all examinations necessitated some degree of compensation which then seriously weakened the inferences about particular skills that were warranted from the final overall grade[1]. The solution adopted throughout the UK was to 'stratify' achievement domains, so that certain parts of the domain were associated with particular grades or levels.

Such methods were investigated intensively during the 1980s during the development of 'grade-related criteria' for the national school-leaving exam-ination (Good and Cresswell, 1988) and many graded or graduated assessment schemes (Foxman, Ruddock and Thorpe, 1989; Graded Assessment in Math-ematics, 1992; Pennycuick and Murphy, 1988).

In some cases (e.g. mathematics) these strata were defined hierarchically so that succeeding strata subsumed earlier levels (psychological strata), while in others (e.g. science) the strata represented a partition of the domain (cur-ricular strata). However, even where the domain has been partitioned (rather than nested), the curricular sequencing is based on an assumed notion of increasing difficulty, so that there is an imposed order among the components of the domain[2].

The curriculum model presented by such stratification of the domain is almost always reflected in the assessment model: each of the marks available in the test can be attributed unambiguously to one of the different levels. The fundamental technical problem in standard-setting, therefore, has been to develop a procedure for determining, for each candidate, which of the 'levels' or grades of the assessment scale best describes the overall performance of the candidate, given, for each level, the proportion of items identified with that level that have been correctly answered by the candidate[3].

The most rigid 'hurdle' approach is to treat each level as independent, and to award the candidate the highest grade or level at which she has attained some fixed proportion of the available marks. Provided the proportion of marks required at each level is sufficiently high (75 per cent or 80 per cent is typical), users of test results are quite justified in concluding that a candidate awarded a particular level has demonstrated most of the achievements associated with that level.

Unfortunately, with such a procedure, a candidate who just fails to achieve the required proportion at each of the levels cannot be given a grade at all. To overcome this difficulty, Long (1985) proposed that marks should be added cumulatively, with multiple cut-scores being set on the single mark scale. Many such models have since been proposed, each of which represents, implicitly, a test-independent model of the performance of a 'minimally competent candidate' at each level. Long himself suggested that the cut score for level n should be set at 80 per cent of the marks at each of the tested levels up to and including level n, while Schagen and Hutchinson of the NFER proposed a cut-score of 100 per cent of all marks for tested levels below level n and 50 per cent of the marks at level n. Based on empirical data from National Curriculum science tests, Massey (1993) proposed that the cut-score for level n should be set by summing 10 per cent, 20 per cent, 30 per cent, 60 per cent, 70 per cent, 75 per cent and 80 per cent of the marks available at level $n+3$, $n+2$, $n+1$, n, $n-1$, $n-2$ and $n-3$ respectively. These three models are illustrated in Figure 7.1.

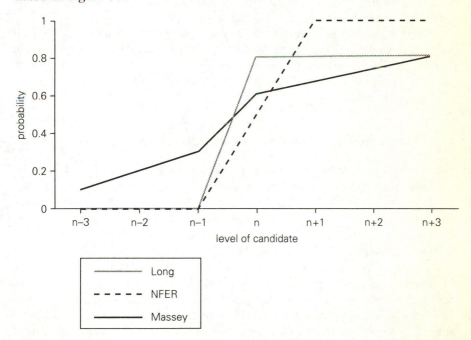

Figure 7.1: Probability of 'minimally competent' students' correct answers

The assumption that all the items associated with a particular level are equally difficult and equally discriminating appears, at first sight to be rather difficult to justify, but provided the models are known to test developers when they begin to develop tests, then fit to the assumed model can be one of the criteria used by developers in selecting items. However, the difficulty with such an approach is that the final test (and therefore the standard) is almost completely determined by the test developers. Although this is common in the UK, such a situation would be regarded as unacceptable in many countries, and as a result, many different test-dependent standard-setting procedures have been devised.

Data-oriented Test-centred Procedures

Several of the standard-setting methods discussed by Berk (1986) can only be used with multiple-choice methods. The only method that is applicable within the constraints of National Curriculum assessment (and which, fortunately, also gets the highest 'approval rating' in Berk's 'consumer's guide') is the procedure that has come to be known as the Angoff procedure (Angoff, 1971).

As usually applied, the Angoff procedure requires a team of judges, working independently, to assign to each item in the test a number between 0 and 1, corresponding to the probability that a 'minimally competent' candidate would be able to answer the question correctly. The judge's probabilities for each item are summed to give a minimally acceptable standard for that judge. The cut-score is then the average of the sums over all the judges.

The danger with such test-centred models is that they can generate standards which appear to be quite reasonable, but, in fact, are almost impossible to achieve. For this reason, there are many procedures that either use normative data explicitly in the original standard-setting, or allow empirical data to influence the cut-score.

Data-oriented Examinee-centred Procedures

According to Jaeger (1989), the most popular examinee-centred models in the US have been the borderline-groups and the contrasting-groups procedures proposed by Zieky and Livingstone (1977). The crucial point about such methods is that they require the allocation of candidates to groups (competent, borderline, inadequate) before the test is administered, and therefore call for some other method of assessment. The borderline-groups procedure defines a standard as the median test-score achieved by the borderline group, while the contrasting groups procedure sets a cut-score so as to maximize the discrimination between the clearly competent and the clearly inadequate groups. The borderline-groups procedure therefore ignores the performance of all those judged to be either competent or inadequate, while the contrasting-groups procedure ignores all those deemed 'borderline'.

In England, models from decision theory have been used to inform the process of setting standards for the school-leaving university entrance examinations. Notable in this respect is the work of the Decision-Analytic Aids to Examining (DAATE) project (French, Wilmott and Slater, 1990).

Comparison of Methods

Many studies have been conducted in which different standard-setting methods are applied to the same test in order to establish the comparability of standards set by different methods. Although the data is difficult to summarize, it does seem that the contrasting-groups and Nedelsky (1954) procedures appear to generate more 'lenient' standards, and that the standard derived from the Angoff method may be the most demanding more often than would be expected by chance variation Jaeger (1989).

One finding does, however, emerge unequivocally: different methods produce different standards! Mills (1983) found that one method generated a standard that rejected nearly thirty times as many students as the other, and Jaeger's (1989) analysis showed that, averaged over thirty-two comparative studies, the cut-score suggested by the most demanding method was over five times the cut-score suggested by the least demanding method.

Glass (1978) interpreted the range of standards suggested by different methods as invalidating the whole idea of 'minimal competence'. Others (e.g. Hambleton, 1980) have argued that because different methods place emphasis on different aspects of performance, the discrepancies arise naturally out of the manifold interpretations that are placed on test results. A summary of the methods discussed is shown in Figure 7.2. No standard-setting method is ideal, but one may support the most important inferences that are likely to be drawn from the results better than the others. This suggests that ideally, several methods should be used, and the resulting cut-scores can be balanced with other (possibly not even measurement-related) factors, when determining a cut-score.

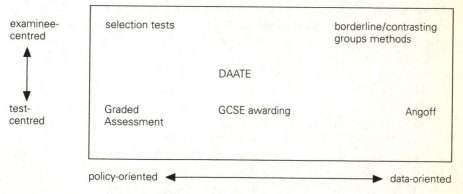

Figure 7.2:   Classification of standard-setting procedures

Applications to National Curriculum Assessment

In order to maximize reliability, some National Curriculum tests will be available in several 'tiers', with each tier covering three levels. Students estimated by their teachers to be at (say) level 6 would sit a test covering levels 5–7 so that the student could be awarded the level above or below that estimated by the teacher with a reasonable degree of reliability.

In National Curriculum assessment, an item relating to (say) level 5 on the eight-point reporting scale could, for example, appear in a test 'tier' covering levels 3–5, a tier covering levels 4–6 and in one for levels 5–7. With such a model of 'overlap' there would be five potential thresholds (in this case the 'minimally acceptable' standards for levels 3, 4, 5, 6 and 7)[4]. Each level 5 item would need to be rated with respect to each of these five thresholds, but once this is done, the same data is used for this item for each tier in which the item appears. In this way the item 'carries its difficulty rating around with it', thus avoiding complex technical problems of equating the standards on the different tiers.

In the original Angoff procedure, there is only a single threshold. Moving to multiple thresholds as required in National Curriculum assessment does not present any new theoretical difficulties, but there is one major practical difficulty.

With a typical National Curriculum test, the number of items and the number of thresholds against which each item is to be rated means that it is unlikely that all judges could rate all items against all thresholds. The question is, therefore, how should the items be allocated to judges? For example, if the judges involved in rating items against the level 4 threshold are different from those rating items against the threshold for level 5, there is the possibility that level 5 might end up being easier than level 4.

However, asking judges to rate the same item at more than one threshold also presents difficulties, since the Angoff method relies on judges holding in their minds an image of the 'minimally competent' student at the threshold in question. Whether judges can do this sufficiently well at more than one threshold, or change from one image to another quickly, is not clear. Several studies (two of which are summarized below) have already been conducted into the appropriateness of Angoff-type procedures for National Curriculum assessment, but much more research on the relative strengths and weaknesses of different experimental designs is needed.

The mathematics tests for 14-year-olds in 1994 covered levels 3–10 in five tiers: 3–5, 4–6, 5–7, 6–8 and 9–10. Early in 1994, twenty-five teachers participated in a two-day conference, using a three-stage Angoff procedure (i.e. initial judgment, followed by normative data, followed by discussion).

When the data were analyzed, a remarkably coherent pattern emerged. The cut-scores set tended to increase linearly according to level (about 20 per cent per level) and to decrease with the tier (so that the cut score for a particular level on one tier was, on average 23 per cent lower than the cut-score for the same level on the tier below. No significant differences were found between the two groups looking at the same levels, but the final cut-scores set were, on average, 6 per cent lower than those set initially (Lundy and Close, 1993).

More recently, Morrison and his colleagues at Queen's University of Belfast found that the normative data has very little influence on the standards set with the Angoff procedure (Morrison, Healy and Wylie, 1994). It seems, therefore, that the opportunity to discuss standards with colleagues is the most important factor in judges' tendencies to revise their initial standards downwards. This suggests that either a two-stage Angoff procedure (initial rating followed by discussion and revision), or a three-stage Angoff procedure, with normative data provided from pre-test and item piloting studies (rather than 'live' normative data) provide a sound basis for setting standards for National Curriculum assessment. Furthermore, in the Belfast study, the inter-rater effects accounted for only 11 per cent of the total variability in scores, confirming the findings from research relating to Angoff-based standard-setting in the US that panels of fifteen to twenty are quite adequate.

However, it is important to note that the foregoing discussion relates to standard-setting for individuals, rather than groups. Although the error attributable to the judges in the standard set is small in comparison to the test error, this will not be true for group data. Over a whole national cohort, the random error due to the test will be negligible[5], but the error due to the judges will remain exactly the same. So if in one year, the cut-score set is towards the lower end of the confidence interval, while the following year it is towards the upper end, then 'standards' within the population could appear to be falling simply due to chance variation in the cut score. This suggests that if year-on-year comparability is required, standard-setting panels should be as large as can be managed. However, the composition of such panels also needs careful consideration if the cut-scores are to reflect the progressive nature of the levels in the reporting scale.

Recommendations for Composition of Panels of Experts

Teachers will obviously be more expert at judging the standards with which they have more experience, but it is necessary that cut-scores relating to levels that are awarded at more than one key stage are set consistently. One way to secure this is to ensure that the expertise of panels setting standards for particular levels is in proportion to the students who are awarded that level (this would, in effect, require that different teachers judge different levels, thus resolving one of the issues raised above).

For example, data on the distribution of attainment derived in Wiliam (1992) would suggest that panels of approximately thirty judges for each level should be constituted as shown in Figure 7.3. In practice, having just two panels — one composed of twenty Key Stage 1, eight Key Stage 2 and two Key

	Level							
	1	**2**	**3**	**4**	**5**	**6**	**7**	**8**
KS1 teachers	27	26	12					
KS2 teachers	3	4	14	20	15	8	3	
KS3 teachers			4	10	15	22	27	30

Figure 7.3:   Suggested constitution of panels of thirty for each level

Stage 3 teachers setting standards for levels 1, 2 and 3, and another composed of ten Key Stage 2 and twenty Key Stage 3 teachers setting standards for levels 4, 5, 6, 7 and 8 — would be a reasonable compromise.

Recommendations for Setting Cut-scores

National Curriculum assessment has a number of priorities all of which need to be given some attention in the setting of standards. However, rather than viewing these (often conflicting) priorities as requiring weights to be attached to them, it may be more helpful to view the priorities as concerns which need to be met. One way to think of these is as a needle on a dial: as long as the needle is not in the 'danger' or 'red' zone, then the standard is acceptable. Examples of such 'constraints' are 'If the cut-score for level 6 is below 57, you'll be able to get level 6 without getting any items correct at levels 6 or above' or 'If the cut-score's over 73, then you'll have to get some level 7 items as well as all the items up to level 6 right to get level 6'.

In order to take account of these multiple objectives for National Curriculum assessment, it seems appropriate that a series of aims be formulated that can be translated into tight criteria. These criteria can then be used to validate the chosen standard. Each criterion will yield a range within which the cut-score should fall. The cut-score would then be the lowest mark that simultaneously satisfies all the conditions. The actual aims and criteria to be used should be determined after consultation, but a preliminary list of four such is given below.

Aim 1:   the standard should be based on a notion of minimum competence.
Criterion: The standard set should be at or below (but no more than two standard errors of measurement below) the cut-score determined by a two or three-stage Angoff procedure.

Aim 2:   the standard for a particular level should relate only to items up to that level.
Criterion: The standard set for a particular level should not require any achievement at a higher level, nor be achievable without some achievement at that level.

Aim 3: the standard for a particular level should relate to the professional and public expectations for that level.

          Criterion: The standard should result in facilities (assessed on the basis of the pre-test data) broadly in line with the facilities suggested in the TGAT (1988) report. For example, the cut scores set should result in facilities for 14-year-olds in the following ranges:

$$93 \leq \text{level } 3 \leq 100$$
$$86 \leq \text{level } 4 \leq 96$$
$$69 \leq \text{level } 5 \leq 79$$
$$45 \leq \text{level } 6 \leq 55$$
$$21 \leq \text{level } 7 \leq 31$$
$$4 \leq \text{level } 8 \leq 14$$

Aim 4: the standard for a particular level in each subject should result in comparable facilities for all subjects.

          Criterion: This will be achieved if a criterion similar to that proposed for aim 3 is implemented. Otherwise some sort of similar criterion will need to be employed. However, it may already be too late. There is already a suggestion that the 'English creep' that resulted in the standards for English in school-leaving examinations being 'easier' than those for mathematics is now affecting National Curriculum assessment!

Conclusion

There are other possible aims, and many might disagree with the operationalizations of those aims in terms of criteria presented above. Nevertheless, it seems to me that the principle of converting aims into criteria that yield precise intervals within which the eventually adopted cut-score must fall is useful. There is clearly no 'best' method, but by attending to a range of concerns, it may be possible to develop standards that pay reasonable heed to the conflicting demands made of National Curriculum assessment.

Notes

1 The use of profiles would of course have helped here but it was clear that there would still be a requirement to represent the overall performance in terms of a single 'brute grade' which would support inferences about particular aspects of performance.

2 While it would therefore be possible in a partitioned (rather than a nested) domain, for a student to acquire 'high-level' skills without necessarily acquiring 'low-level' skills, it is assumed that this will not happen due to the choice of curriculum

sequences. Whether this assumption is warranted has been a source of much debate.

3   It is also possible, of course, that, in the interests of efficient test administration a candidate may not be assessed with respect to each level.

4   In general, with a 'regular' tiering strategy, with 1 level per tier, and p levels of overlap, the number of thresholds against which each item will need to be rated (t) is:

$$l + [(l - 1) / (l - p)] \cdot (l - p)$$

5   For example, in a cohort of 40,000 students, the standard error for cohort's mean would be half of one per cent of the error in each individual's score.

References

ANGOFF, W.H. (1971) 'Scales, norms and equivalent scores', in THORNDIKE, R.L. (Ed) *Educational Measurement*, Washington, DC, American Council on Education, pp. 508–600.

BERK, R.A. (1986) 'A consumer's guide to setting performance standards on criterion-referenced tests', *Review of Educational Research*, **56**, 1, pp. 137–172.

CRESSWELL, M.J. (1994) 'Aggregation and awarding methods for National Curriculum assessments in England and Wales: A comparison of approaches proposed for key stages 3 and 4', *Assessment in Education: Principles, Policy and Practice*, **1**, 1, pp. 45–61.

DES/WO (1988) *Report of the Task Group an Assessment and Testing*, London, DES.

FOXMAN, D.D., RUDDOCK, G.J. and THORPE, J. (1989) *Graduated Tests in Mathematics*, Windsor, UK, NFER-Nelson.

FRENCH, S., WILMOTT, A.S. and SLATER, J.B. (1990) *Decision Analytical Aids to Examining: The DAATE Report*, London, UK, School Examinations and Assessment Council.

GLASS, G.V. (1978) 'Standards and criteria', *Journal of Educational Measurement*, **15**, 4, pp. 237–261.

GOOD, F.J. and CRESSWELL, M.J. (1988) *Grading the GCSE*, London, UK, Secondary Examinations Council.

GRADED ASSESSMENT IN MATHEMATICS (1992) *Complete Pack*, Walton-on-Thames, UK, Thomas Nelson.

HAMBLETON, R.K. (1978) 'On the use of cut-scores with criterion-referenced tests in instructional settings', *Journal of Educational Measurement*, **15**, 4, pp. 277–290.

HAMBLETON, R.K. (1980) 'Test score validity and standard setting methods', in BERK R.A. (Ed) *Criterion-referenced Measurement: The State of the Art*, Baltimore, MD, Johns Hopkins University Press, pp. 80–123.

JAEGER, R.M. (1989) 'Certification of student competence', in LINN, R.L. (Ed) *Educational Measurement*, Washington, DC, American Council on Education/Macmillan, pp. 485–514.

LONG, H.A. (1985, 27 June–2 July) 'Experience of the Scottish Examinations Boards in developing a grade-related criteria system of awards', Paper presented at 11th Annual Conference of the IAEA held at Oxford, UK. Dalkeith, UK, Scottish Examinations Board.

LUNDY, I. and CLOSE, G.S. (1993) 'Experiences in setting cut-offs for key stage mathematics in 1994', unpublished report prepared for School Curriculum and Assessment Authority, London, UK, King's College London Centre for Educational Studies.

MASSEY, A. (1993) 'Criterion-related test development and national assessment standards', unpublished report prepared for School Curriculum and Assessment Authority, Cambridge, UK, University of Cambridge Local Examinations Syndicate.

MESSICK, S. (1989) 'Validity', in LINN, R.L. (Ed) *Educational Measurement*, Washington, DC, American Council on Education/Macmillan, pp. 13–103.

MILLS, C.N. (1983) 'A comparison of three methods of establishing cut-off scores on criterion-referenced tests', *Journal of Educational Measurement*, 20, pp. 283–292.

MORRISON, H.G., HEALY, J. and WYLIE, C. (1994) 'An investigation of the 1994 key stage 3 sample mathematics paper with Angoff-determined cut-scores at levels 3, 4 and 5', unpublished report prepared for School Curriculum and Assessment Authority, Belfast, UK, Queen's University of Belfast.

NEDELSKY, L. (1954) 'Absolute grading standards for objective tests', *Educational and Psychological Measurement*, **14**, 1, pp. 3–19.

PENNYCUICK, D. and MURPHY, R. (1988) *The Impact of Graded Tests*, London, Falmer Press.

ROBITAILLE, D.F. and GARDEN, R.A. (Eds) (1988) *The IEA Study of Mathematics II: Contexts and Outcomes of School Mathematics*, Oxford, UK, Pergamon.

SCHAUB, M. and BAKER, D.P. (1991) 'Solving the math problem: Exploring mathematics achievement in Japanese and American middle grades', *American Journal of Education*, **99**, 4, pp. 623–642.

SECRETARY OF STATE FOR EDUCATION AND SCIENCE (1984) 'Speech to the North of England Conference, in Secondary Examinations Council Annual report 1983–84', London, UK, Secondary Examinations Council, pp. 60–68.

SECRETARY OF STATE FOR EDUCATION AND SCIENCE (1988) Assessment and Testing: A Reply to Mr Key, in Parliamentary Written Answers, Hansard, 7 June 1988, London, UK, Her Majesty's Stationery Office.

WILIAM, D. (1992) 'Special needs and the distribution of attainment in the National Curriculum', *British Journal of Educational Psychology*, 62, pp. 397–403.

ZIEKY, M.J. and LIVINGSTONE, S.A. (1977) *Manual for Setting Standards on the Basic Skills Assessment Tests*, Princeton, NJ, Educational Testing Service.

8   Seeing the Wood through the Trees: Setting Standards in the National Curriculum

Colin Robinson

Summary

The National Curriculum (of England and Wales) is primarily a medium through which the government attempts to involve itself in the education of future generations. For the first time in our history the requirements of what teachers are to teach and what children are to learn are being set out for all to see. The fact that they are so explicit, so public and, unfortunately, so open to different interpretations, makes the setting of standards a very important function. How do we go about it, and are we likely to succeed?

Introduction

In the beginning was the word. Not, in this case, the word of God, but the word of the curriculum Orders. Published over a period of some eighteen months, the Orders represented the combined wisdom of panels of experts: one in each of the ten subjects laid down by law as the Foundation subjects. The problem with words is that they are open to a variety of interpretations and they depend for their meaning on connections they make within the mind of the reader. This results in the same requirements being interpreted in different ways according to the assumptions and prejudgments made by the person interpreting them.

Take a simple requirement. Suppose we require that the pupil is taught to multiply two-digit numbers. What does this mean?

Take any two-digit numbers and you can develop strategies for multiplying them but with some there are different strategies that can be adopted: multiplying by 10, 20 etc. is very different from multiplying by 47. But is 10 × 47 any more difficult than 47 × 10? Does the arrangement of the numbers as follows:

$$
\begin{array}{ccc}
10 & \text{or} & 47 \\
\times\ \underline{47} & & \times\ \underline{10}
\end{array}
$$

make any difference? What is the effect of putting these numbers into a context such as 'How many people are there in forty-seven rows with ten people in each?' Does writing the numbers as words make a difference?

As teachers we know that all these differences do make a difference — at least in the early stages of learning. This does not mean that the children, when learning how to multiply, will always get the sums wrong. What is more likely is that they will be erratic — sometimes getting 'difficult' forms right whilst failing on what we thought were easy.

Progression

In setting out the original National Curriculum, too much credence was given to the idea that we can arrange learning in a hierarchy: starting with the easy things at level 1 and progressing through levels of increasing difficulty. Progression is the stuff of education. The whole of the learning process depends on the learners adding to what they know already. But learning does not follow the same pattern for every learner and, therefore, no single progression will adequately reflect the development of each individual.

Look at some of the hierarchical requirements for mathematics in the 1989 version of the mathematics curriculum — remembering that these statements of attainment defined the attainment target at each level and, as such, had the force of law.

Level 3   Pupil should
- *know and use addition and subtraction number facts to 20 (including zero);*
- *solve problems involving multiplication or division of whole numbers or money, using a calculator where necessary;*
- *know and use multiplication facts up to 5 × 5, and all those in the 2, 5 and 10 multiplication tables.*

Level 4   Pupils should
- *know multiplication facts up to 10 × 10 and use them in multiplication and division problems;*
- *(using whole numbers) add or subtract mentally two 2-digit numbers; add mentally several single-digit numbers; without a calculator add and subtract two 3-digit numbers, multiply a 2-digit number by a single-digit number and divide a 2-digit number by a single-digit number;*
- *solve addition or subtraction problems using numbers with no more than two decimal places; solve multiplication or division problems starting with whole numbers.*

The point about all of these is that they are fine objectives for teaching. They do represent a sort of logical sequence that would make sense — you don't try to teach too much about the 7 or 9 times tables if the children haven't yet grasped the 2, 5 or 10. But if a particular child does grasp the 'more difficult' one first, we are just thankful for the bonus.

Assessment

The problem lies in trying to use these as criteria for assessment. Even if they were perfectly formed criteria which were wholly unambiguous in their meaning, they would still represent inappropriate assessment criteria. The linear progression that they assume is untenable — even within particular strands. If you start to require all of them before a particular level can be awarded, you produce wholly arbitrary results which can only be interpreted as representing the minimum standard attained — a very demotivating feature for the child who has achieved bits and pieces at many levels. So how have we tackled the problem?

Firstly we moved to an assessment regime that tests a very small sample of the domain — completely abandoning the notion of replicating classroom activities that the Task Group on Assessment and Testing put forward in its report (DES/WO, 1988). The sampling is too light to provide the necessary evidence of mastery of a particular statement, so the focus has shifted to the level as a whole.

But even in this shift, the level was still defined by the statements of attainment. The criterion for success was modified in the light of the number of statements tested. This led to even more arbitrary results. If the child happened to be successful on the statements assessed, the level was awarded. But there was no evidence that the statements within a level were sufficiently congruent to justify the assumption that success on those assessed could be taken as an indication that the child would have succeeded on the others. Perhaps even more worryingly, the fact that a child did not succeed on one or more of the assessed statements resulted in the level being denied, when assessment on the other statements might have led to success. Such a procedure could not be defended.

We therefore moved to the use of marks, albeit still trying to make use of the statements of attainment (which, after all, were the legal requirements). The statements were used as a basis for designing the questions and for establishing the cut-scores for the different levels. But now, if the pupil had achieved success on what was deemed a harder question, this could be set against the failure on an easier question. We were progressing towards a method familiar in most examinations.

The obvious next stage was to get rid of the statements of attainment. But they did have a value — as we have seen before — as objectives for teaching. They did set out the 'rules of the game' in a way that we had not previously attempted.

Revised Curriculum

When Sir Ron Dearing undertook his review of the National Curriculum last year, the whole question of the progressive ten-level scale came under scrutiny. Opinion was divided but, in the end, the advantages for teaching were accepted and the scale was retained. What was agreed, however, was that the use of the statements of attainment should be abandoned. They have been replaced by what are called 'level descriptions' whose focus is the whole level, and which are to be used in a completely different way.

Statements of attainment set out to remove from the teacher (acting in the role of assessor) as much of the responsibility for making a judgment as possible. A child was assessed against criteria for the achievement of each statement and, if sufficient statements were achieved, the level would be automatically awarded. If the requisite number had not been 'ticked off', the level could not be awarded. Level descriptions rely on teachers making a judgment. They are to take the child's work as a whole and judge it in comparison with the level descriptions. There are likely to be features in the work that would be better described by the description at one level but others that make one believe that it is best typified by another. This change of use is signalled in the format of the new level descriptions. For example in mathematics at level 3:

> *Pupils have extended their understanding of place value to numbers up to 1000 and approximate these to the nearest 10 or 100. They have begun to use decimals and negative numbers, in contexts such as money, temperature and calculator displays. Pupils use mental recall of addition and subtraction facts up to 20 in solving problems. Pupils use mental recall of the 2, 5 and 10 multiplication tables, and others up to 5 × 5, in solving whole number problems involving multiplication and division, including those which give rise to remainders. They are beginning to develop other mental strategies of their own and use them to find methods for adding and subtracting two-digit numbers. They use calculator methods where appropriate. Pupils also solve problems involving multiplication or division of money by whole numbers.*

No longer do we have the 'bullet points' defining separate requirements. The continuous prose attempts to describe 'typical' performance, without requiring all of it to be displayed.

Setting Standards

So how do we go about setting standards? There is no doubt in my mind that the definition of standards in terms of a progressive scale across the whole of a child's school career is a step forward in recognizing what each part of the educational process is dependent upon and builds on what has gone before. It is therefore appropriate that we articulate that progression in some way, and the ten level scale is not a bad start (even if levels 9 and 10 are a bit difficult to envisage).

The next stage in the process is ensuring that a consensus emerges as to what constitutes performance at each level — balancing superior skills in one area against deficiencies in another to arrive at a level that really does do justice to the child's achievement. Two ways are suggested of achieving this: firstly, the circulation of examples of pupils' work assessed against the parameters of the new level descriptions with a rationale why the assessors decided to award each example a particular level. Secondly, and more importantly, standardization will come through practice: as teachers use their skills to assess their pupils, and exchange views as to the appropriateness of the assessments of their colleagues, a consensus will emerge. It may take a bit of time, but eventually there will be sufficient agreement as to what constitutes 'threeness' or 'fourness' for these to become the lingua franca of the staffroom. We must hope, however, that these terms will be attached to the attainments of the pupils and will not become labels for the pupils themselves, setting ceilings on expectations that have the opposite effect to the increase in standards that we all wish to achieve.

Reference

DES/WO (1988) *Report of the Task Group on Assessment and Testing*, London, DES.

9 Firsts Among Equals: The Case of British University Degrees

Roger Murphy

Summary

Comparability of standards, as represented by national assessment systems, for students in schools in the United Kingdom (UK), has been a major pre-occupation of researchers and policy-makers alike for at least twenty-five years (see for example Forrest and Shoesmith, 1985). The late Desmond Nuttall referred to this obsession with comparability as the 'British disease'. Bob Wood another prominent figure in UK public examinations research, made the following comments in looking back over twenty years of research into that obsession (Wood, 1987).

> Some thought they had the answer (subject pairs, the use of an apti-
> tude test as a control) and stopped looking; the more fastidious simply
> thought the problem insoluble. There were too many reasons why
> results which purported to show comparability, or lack of it might be
> invalid. Towards the end, my ambitions were no higher than looking
> for signs of a kind of 'relaxed' comparability i.e. nothing grotesquely
> out of true. As I read the reports now (Hecker and Wood, 1979;
> Garrett and Wood, 1980) I see how painstakingly we built proviso
> upon proviso, caveat upon caveat, usually starting with how little time
> was available for the exercise. I suppose there was some grim intel-
> lectual pleasure in it.

Chasing after Comparable Assessment Standards

The above quotation sums up quite clearly the dilemma of comparability re-search. When one comes to compare the standard of things that are unlike such as GCSE grades in Chemistry and French then there is very little that can be said other than that they describe very different things. Ultimately this can become the educational equivalent of trying to combine the long jump with the pole vault and the 1500 metres at an athletics meeting and suggesting that the competitors in these events should be seen as competing against each other, and given a single set of results. Different athletics events like these have to be judged separately and any judgment about standards used in one will be inappropriate for another, similarly with different subjects studied within an overall curriculum. Indeed Desmond Nuttall having grappled with the philosophical challenge of between-subjects comparability and having been involved in a number of comparability studies eventually threw in the towel and expressed his misgivings about this venture in an article entitled 'The myth of comparability' (Nuttall, 1979).

Comparability within a subject, say between different boards or alternative syllabuses set by the same board, or between years is likely to be more feasible, especially within the context of national secondary school leaving examinations, being set marked and graded now by only five examination groups. This is especially the case if one is prepared to be content with Wood's (1987) 'relaxed' view of comparability, meaning that there are not huge differences in syllabus content or objectives introduced by individual examination groups. As Nuttall (1979) had it 'comparability can only be rough and ready and is seldom as important as it is made out to be'.

It is likely that the public need to be reassured about comparability of assessment standards may be about to shift from school level education to higher education. A rapid expansion in the numbers of universities in Britain, the increasing numbers of students being admitted to degree courses, and the intense stiffening of competition for jobs are all contributing to a situation where searching questions are starting to be asked about the relative standards of different degree courses. In this chapter I want to take an exploratory look at this under-researched issue and attempt to map out some possible ways of moving forward.

Satisfying the Need for Comparable Standards

What is certainly clear is that within a society, where education is highly valued and access to further educational opportunities and certain highly rewarded careers depends upon results, there is a need for a simple and common understanding of educational assessment results. Using common grading scales, for National Curriculum assessments, GCSE and A-level examinations and university degree courses, provides the impression of simple straightforward comparable standards upon which quick choices and decisions can be made about future opportunities for individuals. A good set of GCSE grades is a passport to post-16 schooling. Three good A-levels grades is a passport to a wide range of University degree courses. A good University degree is a passport to certain postgraduate courses and/or career options.

All of this works fine until concern arises about the equivalence of these apparently similar qualifications. Are GCSE results the same standard as O-level results? Are A-level grades from Board X the same standard as grades from Board Y? Is a first class honours degree from the University of Skelmersdale the same as one from Oxford University? Questions like these are hard enough even before one gets into asking the even more complex between-subject questions.

Largely speaking, concerns over the comparability of school level assessments appear to have subsided somewhat in recent years. A greatly diminished number of examination boards, clearer guidelines about common elements in syllabus construction, a code of conduct laid down for the boards to follow, and regular national quality checks have all helped to make it clear that all that can be done is being done. Most people also accept that achievements in different subject areas require different skills and competences, and therefore a common grading scale can be seen as a shorthand way of summarizing achievement in relation to the demands of the subject studied.

The situation in higher education, however, is far more complicated and with more and more talk about 'market forces' and 'competition' in education there will be an even greater desire to ask questions about what individual universities are offering in different subject areas and the relative standards of the degrees they award.

University Degree Standards Come Under Scrutiny

Higher education in Britain has gone through various phases of expansion during the last thirty years, and there are now ninety-two independent universities with powers to award their own degrees. Despite a fairly widespread public recognition that such a diverse system of mass higher education must contain very different opportunities for students, types of courses, and ultimately outcome standards, there is a reluctance from the government to acknowledge this.

The Secretary of State for Education in a speech to the Higher Education Funding Council for England (HEFCE) Conference on 12 April 1994 called for the 'gold standard' of British University degrees to be maintained. Having commended the broader work of the Higher Education Quality Council (HEQC) he called for them to focus their efforts more specifically on comparability issues.

> There is evidence that many institutions have found the HEQC audits very helpful, and we have seen progress in strengthening internal quality control systems. In my view, which I have shared with HEQC representatives in informal discussions, the HEQC ought now to place more emphasis on broad comparability in the standards of degrees offered by different institutions. I know there is much debate about whether it is feasible to do this, or even whether, in a diverse system, it matters. Let me nail my colours to the mast, and say that I think it does, and that we are short-changing students if we suggest otherwise.

> If it is true — as some allege — that examiners have become less demanding recently, then it is the academic community who would be the losers. Their reputation both at home and overseas would rightly suffer. (John Patten, Secretary of State for Education, 12 April 1994)

Threatened with the prospect of externally imposed assessment standards, possibly utilizing developments in the setting of assessment standards developed through initiatives such as National Vocational Qualification (NVQ), the universities are currently trying to strengthen their own claim to be addressing quality matters including the standard of university awards. The Committee of Vice-Chancellors and Principals (CVCP), in July 1994, issued an eleven point plan 'to guarantee the standards of awards' (CVCP, 1994). This plan 'is aimed at developing more efficient assessment procedures and performance indicators that will satisfy the funding councils' responsibility for public funds and provide even more information to students and employers about quality in universities.'

Just what will emerge from all of this activity is difficult to see, but it is noticeable how the problem appears to be being addressed from first principles rather than paying attention, for example, to the recommendations of a major national survey of assessment issues in higher education by Atkins, Beattie and Dockrell (1993) or other significant projects, relating to this matter, such as the work on learning outcomes in higher education by Otter (1992).

It is also the case that the whole area of comparability of standards in higher education in Britain is very under-researched. There is little to go on other than published statistics which reveal facts such as the following:

1   students entering some universities in 1991/92 were five times as likely to get a first class honours degree than those entering others;
2   Cambridge University awarded first class honours degrees to 24 per cent of its graduates in 1993/94. This is 10 per cent higher than any other university;
3   over a ten year period (1983/94 — 1993/94) the average proportion of students awarded first class honours degrees in all the universities has risen every year going from 6.0 per cent to 9.3 per cent in 1993/94.

Of course nothing categoric can be concluded from such statistics but they do raise interesting questions that are worthy of further investigation. It would be very interesting for example, to get sets of external examiners together in a number of subject areas and get them to conduct cross-moderation exercises of the type that have become common in public examinations research. Such exercises will never come out with precise results, but in a context where there is interest in comparing standards they can provide a productive way of investigating the issue. They can also have a training function in exposing individual institutions to the assessment procedures and standards being applied in other institutions.

	Purpose	Institution responsible	Focus
1.	Quality control	Individual HEIs	Systems and procedures
2.	Quality improvement	Individual HEIs	Subject course
3.	Academic audit	HEQC	Systems procedures (individual institution)
4.	Quality assurance	HEFC	Subject discipline (across institutions)
5.	Professional accreditation	Professional body	Subject course (individual institution)
6.	Standards	External examiners	Subject course (individual institution)

Figure 9.1: Quality assurance in the UK
Source: Green, 1993

The universities are already establishing procedures for quality assurance, in a much wider sense, but it is again apparent that the major emphasis of current quality assessments is on general processes and procedures in universities rather than standards achieved by graduating students. This is a point that came out very clearly from the recent December 1993 Coopers and Lybrand review of HEQC quality audits (Coopers and Lybrand Report, 1993).

> . . . as institutions' missions, student intakes and approaches to teaching and learning become increasingly diverse, there is now growing concern that the previous common understanding of what comprises quality and standards and therefore what are the most appropriate methods of quality control is no longer to be found.

Green (1993) in a helpful overview of quality assurance activities going on in higher education in Western Europe shows how in the UK the range of new quality procedures barely touch upon the question of the standard of degree awards (see Figure 9.1 above). This issue remains as it always has in the hands of a system operated by external examiners, whose role is not connected in any way with the increasingly complex system of quality audits and assessments.

Demonstrating the Comparability of University Assessment Standards

At one level it is possible to understand the desire of vice-chancellors to defend the broad comparability of their institutions' assessment standards. To express doubts about the comparability of these standards leaves the way open for the autonomy of individual institutions to be threatened. One can easily envisage a scenario where a National Curriculum could be required for higher education, along similar lines to the one recently introduced into schools. This could involve attainment targets, benchmark tests, and a national university level system of examinations. Ultimately this type of literal comparability more or less has to be brought about by imposing uniformity on what is otherwise an increasingly diverse system of institutions, entry requirements, courses, teaching methods and assessment methods. The challenge then becomes whether reasonable comparability can be achieved through constrained but reasonable diversity. Such a debate can move us perilously close to a position that is likely to compromise the very concept of universities, as autonomous institutions encouraging freedom of thought and ideas.

The HEQC are currently undertaking various studies of the external examiner system which is the linchpin of any current claims for reasonable comparability of standards. This is again curious in the light of the major study of external examiners that was conducted by a team headed by David Warren-Piper in the 1980s, but which was never published. There can be few who believe that external examiners can do other than modify the most extreme deviations in assessment standards between institutions, especially where their limited time can often be channelled towards resolving a small number of 'borderline cases'. Even at this stage John Stoddart, the chairman of the HEQC, is on record as saying that,

> Changes are needed because the external examiner system, for example, was devised in different times and does not bear scrutiny with the number of students we now have. (*The Times*, 18 July 1994)

It is certainly possible that the role of external examiners could be strengthened, both through a closer specification of effective ways of utilizing their efforts, and by the provision of training and support for them. Many who sought to take this role seriously have, in the past, been thwarted by a lack of information, or a lack of time to digest it, or an involvement only in grade awarding procedures which cannot rectify deficits either in the assessment system, or the course as taught to the students. Elsewhere, along with others, I have developed some ideas about this issue (Murphy, 1989), and there is a good deal of progress that could be made if it is agreed that the external examiner system is the way forward in future development work.

The other strategy currently being pursued by the HEQC is an attempt to explore the specification of so-called 'threshold standards'. According to John Stoddart these will be the basics in the main subjects which could be combined with other more general personal skills that could be seen to be developed through a wide range of university degree courses. All of this is reminiscent of attempts to introduce criterion-referencing of national standards first into GCSE (Murphy, 1986), and then some years later into the National Curriculum

(Murphy, 1994). Neither episode holds out a great deal of hope for the even more complex world of higher education degree courses. Threshold standards may provide some reassurance to a concerned public, but if they only relate to part of what is being assessed they are unlikely to provide a firm foundation for overall comparability of standards. It will be easier to reach agreement about such standards in some areas rather than others, and in my view any such development should be approached with caution.

The Way Ahead

The current system of mass higher education in Britain is providing a diverse array of opportunities to an increasingly large cohort of students. There is in my view no way that this is reconcilable with simplistic notions of comparability, which suggest that the achievements of students awarded the same degree classification in any of ninety-two institutions can be treated as having demonstrated the same educational achievement.

There are however some specific skills and abilities which are commonly acquired by students by the end of this time in higher education, such as certain verbal, quantitative, logical thinking and presentational skills which could be assessed and accreditated through processes more like those developed in NVQ, GNVQ etc. It is possible, therefore, to see ways in which some of the higher levels of NVQs could start to form part of what is assessed in higher education. Such accreditation could usefully complement rather than necessarily replace degree classifications. Such a development could fit into the emerging interest in records of achievement in a number of universities, as a way of being more specific about aspects of student achievement (Trowler and Hinett, 1994; Murphy *et al.*, 1993). Meanwhile, the assessment procedures operated by individual institutions need to be given renewed attention, not least because of the demands of increasingly complex systems of modularization, credit accumulation and transfer, the accreditations of prior learning, and the franchising of university courses to other institutions (see the Robertson Report, 1994). University lecturers now need to be encouraged to become more knowledgeable about educational assessment matters. Assessment standards and procedures need to be made more explicit, and in a situation of diminishing resources, the resources available to ensure that adequate assessment procedures are maintained need to be protected.

Above all, it seems to be pointless to assume that public confidence in the value of university education can only be maintained by asserting that university degree standards are equivalent whichever of the ninety-two institutions, or the numerous departments within them, a student studies at. The reality is that university degrees even in the same subject taken in the same university at the same time may involve the study of different options (or modules) which lead to very different learning outcomes. Students coming off such courses with similar results can only in a very broad sense be thought to have equivalent results. Part of the value of education, and perhaps to an even greater extent higher education, lies in the diversity of opportunity it provides to learners with different interests, abilities and enthusiasms. The cause of raising educational standards has little to do with attempts to make degree results mean the same thing whichever course a student follows.

Finally a distinction needs to be made between vocationally oriented courses in areas such as medicine, nursing, midwifery, law, social work and education, where professional bodies are already starting to prescribe specific standards to be met, and other degree courses where greater diversity of outcomes may be more appropriate (Worth-Butler, Murphy and Fraser, 1994). The professional training function of higher education will properly continue to need to meet widely agreed national standards. In other subject areas, confidence in the overall quality of the system is more important than an over-mechanistic approach to defining and setting assessment standards.

This paper has been published in the British Journal of Curriculum and Assessment (1995), subsequent to the CFAS/EARLI conference.

References

ATKINS, M.J., BEATTIE, J. and DOCKRELL, W.B. (1993) *Assessment Issues in Higher Education*, Sheffield, Employment Department.

COOPERS AND LYBRAND REPORT (1993) *Higher Education Quality Council. Review of Quality Audit*, London, Coopers and Lybrand.

CVCP (1994) 'National Assurance of Quality and Standards in Teaching and Learning', an eleven point plan from the Committee of Vice-Chancellors and Principals.

FORREST, G.M. and SHOESMITH, D.J. (1985) *A Second Review of GCE Comparability Studies*, Manchester, JMB.

GREEN, D. (1993) 'Quality assurance in Western Europe — Trends, practices and issues', *Quality Assurance in Education*, **1**, 3, pp. 4–14.

MURPHY, R.J.L. (1986) 'The emperor has no clothes: Grade criteria and the GCSE', in GIPPS, C. (Ed) *GCSE: An Uncommon Exam*, Bedford Way Papers No 29, University of London Institute of Education.

MURPHY, R.J.L. (1989) 'The role of external examiners in improving student assessments', *External Examining of Undergraduate Psychology Degrees*, British Psychological Society Occasional Paper No 6.

MURPHY, R.J.L. (1994) 'Dearing: A farewell to criterion-referencing?', *British Journal of Curriculum and Assessment*, **4**, 3, pp. 10–12.

MURPHY, R.J.L., MAHONEY, P., JONES, J. and CALDERHEAD, J. (1993) 'Profiling in initial teacher training', *Teacher Development*, **2**, 3, pp. 141–146.

NUTTALL, D.L. (1979) 'The myth of comparability', *Journal of the NAIEA*, **11**, pp. 16–18.

OTTER, S. (1992) *Learning Outcomes in Higher Education: A Development Project Report*, London, UDACE.

PATTEN, J. (1994) *Secretary of State for Education, speech to Higher Education Funding Council*, London, 12 April.

ROBERTSON REPORT (1994) *Choosing to Change: Extending Access, Choice and Mobility in Higher Education*, London, HEQC.

STODDAR, J. (1994) 'Change to the system of external examing', *The Times*, 18 July.

TROWLER AND HINETT (1994) 'Implementing the recording of achievement in higher education', *Capability*, **1**, 1, pp. 53–61.

WOOD, R. (1987) *Measurement and Assessment in Education and Psychology*, Lewes, Falmer Press.

WORTH-BUTLER, M.M., MURPHY, R.J.L. and FRASER, D.M. (1994) 'Towards an integrated model of competence in midwifery', *Midwifery* (In Press).

Test Issues

10 Threats to the Stability of Reported Levels in the National Curriculum

David Dean

Summary

Do National Curriculum assessments provide national standards? Does a level 5 in mathematics at Key Stage 2 represent a different standard to a level 5 in the same subject at Key Stage 3? If that is found to be the case how can reported levels based on National Curriculum assessment claim to have any validity?

Introduction

In 1994 the Further Education Unit (FEU) embarked upon what was inappropriately called the Diagnostic Assessment Project. The aim, in response to 'Unfinished Business' (OFSTED, 1993), was to help Further Education (FE) colleges to identify the most appropriate courses for their post-16 intake. This needs assessment exercise was to investigate the use by the FE sector of a battery of diagnostic instruments and aptitude measures, including tests of literacy and numeracy.

There is an alarming implication. Students entering FE courses such as General National Vocational Qualification (GNVQ) have completed eleven years of compulsory education. It is, therefore, reasonable to expect that a wealth of evidence concerning prior learning experiences and attainment has been well documented. Why does the FE sector not use this existing assessment information? This chapter suggests that the problems evident at the Year Eleven / FE interface are not unique. There appears to exist across all phases of our education system a reluctance to trust and use evidence gathered by other professionals. As children pass from class to class meticulously maintained records of attainment, all immensely time consuming and adding to the teacher's load, are passed to the next teacher only to find that the evidence is put to little use.

This situation should no longer exist. A major thrust of the report of the Task Group on Assessment and Testing (TGAT) (DES, 1988) was the recommendation of a common, progressive curriculum with its associated ten level scale of attainment common to primary and secondary phases.

An important feature of that design is the ease of transition that it was meant to facilitate from class to class or from school to school. Educational achievement is now capable of communication with a reliability and content validity hitherto absent. Assessment data tells a teacher what it is that a child 'knows, understands and can do' and further educational experiences can then be planned accordingly to build upon these achievements — the formative purpose of assessment. This is the cornerstone of TGAT. The aim of this chapter is to examine its reality. Do National Curriculum assessments provide national, trustworthy, standards? If a Key Stage 2 level 5 represents a different standard from a Key Stage 3 level 5, then one of the central tenets of the National Curriculum is seriously flawed. There are a number of potential threats to the comparability or stability of reported subject attainment arising from the current (1994) National Curriculum assessment arrangements. The question of comparability between key stages is considered, as is the threat to stability of outcomes within key stages which results from the tier structure.

Criteria and Standards in the National Curriculum

The mechanism through which the TGAT model was to be realized was the establishment of a progressive ten level scale in which a child's attainment is measured against well-defined learning objectives. This is not an entirely new concept. The objectives movement of the 1920s (Charters, 1923) built upon the work of management training (Taylor, 1912) but quickly collapsed under the weight of the exponentially increasing numbers of objectives as the curriculum was broken down into its constituent elements. Reliability could only be ensured by the removal of any ambiguity and so the curriculum had to be defined in infinitesimal detail. See Pendleton's 1,581 objectives for English in Davies (1976). This notion was resurrected by Tyler and his student Bloom (1956) and gained further credence as criterion referenced measurement, a term first coined by Glaser (1963) in which a child's attainment was measured against a set of 'well defined competencies'.

Here lies the rub. Since a complete specificity of definition is too un-wieldy, the model of criterion referenced assessment adopted is a mixture of specific objectives and domain referenced with both open and closed do-mains. The curriculum is in the hands of those charged with the responsibility of delivering it and there is therefore recognition of the teachers' professional expertise and a certain degree of interpretation of the statements of attainment. The Centre for Formative Assessment Studies (CFAS), since its early work on developing Key Stage 1 core subject SATs through the Standard Tests and Assessment Implementation Research (STAIR) consortium (1989–90), has argued the case for national assessment procedures as an effective means of commun-icating common and consistent interpretations of Statements of Attainment, and hence promulgating common and consistent national standards (Sadler, 1987).

Comparability Between Key Stages

The research exercise described here examines the consistency achieved across the 1994 mathematics Standard Assessment Tests for Key Stages 2 and 3 in England and Wales. It investigates comparability between the attainments of Year 6 pupils in the final year of primary school (age 11) and Year 9 pupils in the third year of secondary school (age 14).

Structure of the Mathematics Tests at Key Stages 2 and 3

Mathematics tests A and B for Key Stage 2 in 1994 assessed levels 3, 4 and 5. Children with learning difficulties for whom this testing was thought inappropriate completed Assessment Tasks at levels 1 and 2. Extension material (Test C) was also available to assess level 6. The mathematics tests for Key Stage 3 in 1994 were designed to broadly match pupil capabilities by grouping the items in four 'level bands' or tiers. Each tier covered three levels with two overlapping levels from one tier to the next. Decisions about tier entry for pupils were made by at the school level. This structure is illustrated in Table 10.1 (Key Stage 2) and Table 10.2 (Key Stage 3). The focus of the CFAS investigation into between key stage comparability was Papers A and B (Key Stage 2) and Tests 1 and 2 of Tier 3–5 (Key Stage 3). Before a re-testing exercise was carried out a desk review revealed differences in question design and test structure between the two key stages.

Table 10.1: Key Stage 2 tests

	levels 1 and 2	level 3	level 4	level 5	level 6
Special needs tasks	X				
Tests A and B		X	X	X	
Test C (Extension material)					X

Table 10.2: Key Stage 3 tests

	level 2	level 3	level 4	level 5	level 6	level 7	level 8	levels 9 and 10
Special needs tasks	X							
Tier 3–5		X	X	X				
Tier 4–6			X	X	X			
Tier 5–7				X	X	X		
Tier 6–8					X	X	X	
Extension material								X

Sampling the Curriculum

There are some clear design and structural differences between the KS2 and KS3 tests for levels 3 to 5. The KS3 tests distribute marks equally between the three levels and four attainment targets whereas the KS2 tests are weighted towards level 3 and Ma2. Detailed distributions of marks across levels and attainment targets are shown in Table 10.3 (KS2) and Table 10.4 (KS3). The distribution of marks across levels across key stage tests is summarized for comparison in Table 10.5. The effect is that 'level 5 pupils' have more opportunities to drop irrelevant marks (i.e. level 3 and 4) and fewer opportunities to gain relevant marks in KS3. The expected consequence is that level 5 will be less accessible in KS3 tests than in KS2 tests.

Table 10.3: Distribution of marks in KS2 Tier 3–5 tests

	level 3	level 4	level 5	**TOTAL**
AT2	14	10	8	**32**
AT3	7	9	7	**23**
AT4	9	7	7	**23**
AT5	7	8	.7	**22**
TOTAL	**37**	**34**	**29**	**100**

Note: (total marks = 100)

Table 10.4: Distribution of marks in KS3 Tier 3–5 tests

	level 3	level 4	level 5	**TOTAL**
AT2	8.3	8.3	8.3	**25**
AT3	8.3	8.3	8.3	**25**
AT4	8.3	8.3	8.3	**25**
AT5	8.3	8.3	8.3	**25**
TOTAL	**33.3**	**33.3**	**33.3**	**100**

Note: Papers 1 and 2 by percentage

Table 10.5: Percentages of marks for each level in Tier 3–5 tests

	KS2	KS3
level 3	37	33
level 4	34	33
level 5	29	33

There are also differences between key stages in the sampling of the mathematics domain. The differences are summarized in Table 10.6. This clearly demonstrates that Key Stage 2 places an emphasis on number skills with 32 per cent of the marks awarded for Ma2 (Number).

Table 10.6: *Percentages of marks by AT in Tier 3–5 tests*

	KS2	KS3
Ma2	32	25
Ma3	23	25
Ma4	23	25
Ma5	22	25

Question Design: Interpretations of the Mathematics Curriculum

The clearest illustration of differences in standards due to question design and curriculum interpretations arises from the treatment of Attainment Target 5 (Handling Data).[1] Attainment Target 5 has two distinct strands, statistics and probability. The relevant Statements of Attainment are presented in Table 10.7. Differences in outcomes from the tests for KS2 and KS3 may result from different emphases placed on the two strands. The allocation of marks for each of the strands is shown in Table 10.8. The Key Stage 3 tests not only include a higher proportion of probability tasks, but they also require answers in the form of written explanations. Examination of pupil responses carried out by CFAS (CFAS/SCAA, 1994a) reveal higher item difficulty for the probability questions than the statistics questions. This may well be a feature of Key Stage 3 tests placing a demand upon written answers, but the consequence is an obvious absence of comparability.

Table 10.7: *AT5 SoA at levels 3–5 (1994)*

		Statistics		Probability
Level 3	3a	access information in a simple database	3c	use appropriate language to justify decisions when placing events in order of likelihood
	3b	construct and interpret statistical diagrams		
Level 4	4a	interrogate and interpret data in a computer database	4d	estimate and justify the probability of an event
	4b	conduct a survey on an issue of their choice		
	4c	use the mean and range of a set of data		
Level 5	5a	use a computer database to draw conclusions	5d	use an appropriate method for estimating probabilities
	5b	design and use an observation sheet to collect data		
	5c	interpret statistical diagrams		

Table 10.8: Allocation of marks by strand

KS2 Tests Statistics strand	KS2 Tests Probability strand	KS3 Tests Statistics strand	KS3 Tests Probability strand
5/3a interpret frequency chart (3 marks)	5/3c estimate likelihood (2 marks)	5/3a interpret table (4 marks)	5/3c explain probabilities (6 marks)
5/3b add column to bar chart (2 marks)	5/4 estimate and justify probabilities (3 marks)	5/4b plan survey (4 marks)	5/4d explain and calculate probabilities (6 marks)
5/4c make inferences from a statement which gives mean and range (5 marks)		5/5d interpret graphs (4 marks)	
	5/5d estimate probabilities (2 marks)		5/5d explain and calculate probabilities (6 marks)
5/5c interpret graphs (5 marks)			
15 marks	7 marks	12 marks	18 marks

The Importance of Cut-off Scores for the Award of Levels

Since the abandonment of the notion of an aggregation model of attainment building towards a mastery profile, National Curriculum tests are reliant upon the cut-off score model. A consequence is that a reported level of attainment in the subject bears little relationship to the pupils' mastery of the components of the curriculum at that level. Any difference between tests for the different key stages in the model for the determination of cut-off scores is a further threat to comparability. Scrutiny of the cut-off scores for the Key Stage 2 and 3 mathematics tests reveals such inconsistencies.

Effect of Marks Distributions and Cut-off Scores

Table 10.5 showed a slight weighting towards level 3 in the KS2 tests. This combines with lower cut-off scores to produce higher outcomes for some pupils. The cut-off scores are illustrated in Table 10.9. The difference is most marked for the award of level 3 which requires 32.5 per cent of all marks at KS3 but only 24 per cent of marks at KS2. This can have the effect of shifting pupils who are close to boundary scores into a higher level when they take the KS2 tests.

Table 10.9: Comparison of cut-off scores for the award of levels

	KS2 Boundary scores (%) for the award of levels	KS3 Boundary scores (%) for the award of levels
Level 2	12	15.8
Level 3	24	32.5
Level 4	50	55.0
Level 5	73	72.5

The magnitude of this effect was investigated in June 1994 (CFAS/SCAA, 1994b) with sixty-seven Year 9 pupils from four schools who were volunteered to sit the Key Stage 2 tests (Tests A and B) as well as their own Key Stage 3 tests (Tier 3–5, Papers 1 and 2). The main points to emerge from the exercise were:

- from sixty-seven data sets, each of four test papers, forty-two pupils (twenty-four boys, eighteen girls), i.e. 62.7 per cent, achieved the same level in the KS2 retests as they had in the KS3 tests;
- seventeen pupils (eleven boys, six girls), i.e. 25.4 per cent, scored one level higher on the KS2 tests than on the KS3 tests;
- eight pupils (eight boys), i.e. 11.9 per cent, recorded one level lower on the KS2 retests than on the KS3 tests;
- one pupil (a girl) recorded two levels higher (KS3/level 3 — KS2/level 5) on the KS2 tests;
- one pupil (a girl) appeared as recorded two levels lower (KS3/level 2 — KS2/no level) because her KS2 total (11 marks) was in the 0–11 boundary for a 'no level awarded';
- one pupil (a girl) appeared as recorded three levels higher on the KS2 retests because her KS3 total (14 marks) was in the 'no level awarded' category.

A summary of the effects of mark totals and cut-off scores is shown in the scatter plot on Figure 10.1. To demonstrate the magnitude of this effect the

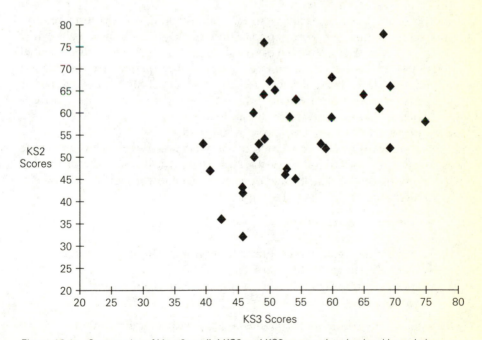

Figure 10.1:   *Scatter plot of Year 9 pupils' KS2 and KS3 scores showing level boundaries*

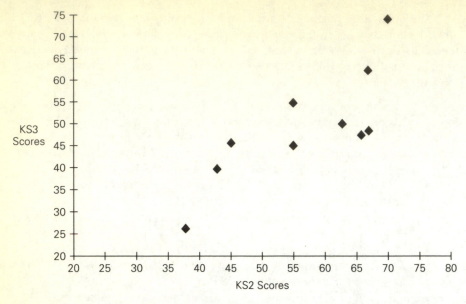

Figure 10.2: Scatter plot of Year 6 pupils' KS3 and KS2 scores showing level boundaries

data from one secondary school (N = 28) is shown as a scatter plot in Figure 10.1 which shows that eleven of the twenty-eight pupils are awarded a higher level on the Key Stage 2 tests.

This is not a feature exclusive to KS3 pupils taking the KS2 tests. A small opportunistic sample of Year 6 pupils undertook a similar resit of the Key Stage 3 tests. The data from the Year 6 cohort taking the KS3 tests is illustrated in Figure 10.2 where a similar trend is observed. The quantitative comparison was complemented by a qualitative review of scripts of the twenty-five pupils (37.3 per cent) who were awarded different levels. The purpose was to investigate whether discrepancies were due to Key Stage 2 setting too low a standard or Key Stage 3 setting too severe a standard.

One such case study concerned a boy who was awarded level 4 by the Key Stage 2 tests and level 3 by the Key Stage 3 tests. Scrutiny of his test papers reveals certain deficits that are not compatible with level 4 attainment. On the evidence of the tests, the pupil:

- cannot solve problems with a calculator
- has no concept of bearings
- cannot deal with inputs and outputs from a simple function machine
- is unable to calculate perimeter
- does not know the conventions of a co-ordinate system
- cannot use a probability scale.

All of these are requirements of the level 4 Programmes of Study, which suggests that the award of level 4 is therefore premature.

Stability of Assessment Outcomes Within a Key Stage

The test structure employed by SCAA in 1994 of arranging the questions in tiers of three levels can itself lead to instability in level outcomes. A pupil's reported level depends upon the tier for which the pupil is entered. The CFAS evaluation of Key Stage 3 tests revealed a higher probability of a pupil gaining one level through entry to a lower tier. This paradox needs explanation.

Consider a pupil whose 'true level' is best described as a solid level 5. Such a pupil might obtain around 90 per cent of the marks for level 4, 70 per cent of level 5 marks, 40 per cent of level 6 and 15 per cent of level 7. Such a profile is plausible and consistent with the findings of the KS3 evaluation. In the absence of rules the school decides the tier of entry for its pupils. The 'solid level 5' pupil might be entered for the 4–6 tier or perhaps the teacher, with some evidence of level 6 attainment from classwork might enter the pupil for the 5–7 tier. Table 10.10 shows the impact of this decision. There is a cynical message in this for schools wanting to play the system in order to enhance potential league table positions.

Table 10.10: *Example of a plausible pupil profile*

	level 4 Marks/40	level 5 Marks/40	level 6 Marks/40	level 7 Marks/40	Tier Total Marks/120	Outcome level
All levels	36	29	16	7		
tier 4–6	36	29	16		81	**6**
tier 5–7		29	16	7	52	**5**

Effect of Tiering Arrangements

Distributions of outcomes levels for the four tiers, and for all tiers combined, are given in Table 10.11. The overall frequencies of levels are broadly in line with expectations. However, the sharp drop from level 6 to level 7 is the one surprising feature. It may well be that we are observing a ceiling effect in terms of pupil ability which has nothing to do with tiering arrangements. It is noted that, for tiers 4–6 and 5–7, the middle level of the tier is the mode level. In

Table 10.11: *Tier effects: Levels achieved*

level	Tier 3–5	Tier 4–6	Tier 5–7	Tier 6–8	All tiers
No award	1	1	0	1	3
2	35				35
3	192	33			225
4	102	167	2		271
5	35	214	62	10	321
6		69	177	124	370
7			103	88	191
8				29	29

Tier 3–5 however the distribution is heavily skewed towards level 3. In the absence of level tasks there is nowhere else to place those pupils who are expected to attain level 3. This means that such pupils are entered in a test in which two thirds of the marks are theoretically beyond their reach. This assumes that the test meets its design specification and the items are broadly in line with the target level. The arrangement must surely have an adverse effect upon level 3 pupils and cannot be deemed satisfactory.

The strategy of placing pupils in the tier whose middle level coincides with Teacher Assessment appears to have been used by most teachers when allocating pupils to tiers 4–6 and 5–7.

There were a number a hopeful level 6 entries to tier 6–8 which may have backfired, if the intention was to give the pupils the maximum chance of a level 7 outcome. A better chance of attaining level 7 is offered in the tier 5–7 tests where level 7 can be obtained with success in only 30 per cent of the level 7 marks (Table 10.12). Contrast this with the profile required to attain level 7 from tier 6–8 when performance at levels 6 and 7 is maintained (Table 10.13). 35 per cent of the level 8 marks are now required in order to reach the level 7 cut-off score. A more normal profile for attaining level 7 from tier 6–8 (Table 10.14) places greater demands on the pupils at levels 6 and 7.

Table 10.12: Possible profile of level 7 attainment from Tier 5–7

	Marks available	Marks obtained	Percentage of level marks
level 5	40	37	92.5
level 6	40	32	80.0
level 7	40	12	30.0
Total	120	81	

Table 10.13: Possible profile of level 7 attainment from Tier 6–8

	Marks available	Marks obtained	Percentage of level marks
level 6	40	32	80
level 7	40	12	30
level 8	40	14	35
Total	120	58	

Table 10.14: Normal profile of level 7 attainment from Tier 6–8

	Marks available	Marks obtained	Percentage of level marks
level 6	40	36	90
level 7	40	16	40
level 8	40	6	30
Total	120	58	

Conclusion

Evidence gathered in 1994 clearly supports the view that subject levels reported as outcomes from the Key Stage 2 and Key Stage 3 national tests in mathematics do not communicate the same standard. The tests are not comparable due to differences in both content (different questions) and structure (application of different cut scores). There are also differences in standards within Key Stage 3 due to the tier structure. The establishment of common standards so that a subject level resulting from national tests carries greater confidence may be achieved by one of two routes, namely enhanced quality control of existing procedures or improved design of testing arrangements.

There is scope for improved comparability between key stages within the existing arrangements by adherence to quality assurance procedures. If we wish to remain faithful to the notion that a level 5 is a level 5 regardless of the age and key stage of the pupil there is a question mark over the rationale for using different tests. The adoption of, for example, a common National Curriculum mathematics test for levels 3–5 would ensure between key stage comparability.

Within Key Stage 3 the tier of entry has a significant impact on the pupil outcome. If the grouping of questions into tiers spanning levels is to persist then it follows that there should be a strong steer to teachers in the form of an entry rule which indicates the use of Teacher Assessment to enter pupils in the most appropriate tier. Pupils expected to attain no higher than level 3 outcome should be entered for levelled tasks rather than the tier 3–5 tests and others should be entered for the tier in which the median level is the Teacher Assessment level. The suggested entry rule is summarized in Table 10.15.

Table 10.15: Entry rule for allocating pupils to tests/tasks

Teacher Assessment	Test to be used
level 2 or 3	levelled tasks
level 4	tier 3–5
level 5	tier 4–6
level 6	tier 5–7
level 7	tier 6–8
level 8	tier 6–8

A radical alternative to the current tier arrangements would be shorter single level tests administered and marked separately. Mastery of a level of attainment could therefore be confirmed and if a pupil's results indicated the possibility of success at a higher level then the higher level test could be administered. While this would be more complex for schools, it removes the possibility of level 5 being awarded to a pupil who attains only 17.5 per cent of the level 5 marks available on the 1994 arrangements.

Note

1 Whilst the terms Attainment Target and Statement of Attainment refer to the National Curriculum in operation at the time of the 1994 tests the arguments are relevant to any test designed by sampling a prescribed curriculum.

References

BLOOM, B.S. (1956) *Taxonomy of Educational Objectives*, New York, US, McKay.

BOBBITT, J.F. (1924) *How to Make a Curriculum*, Boston, Massachusetts, US, Houghton Miflin.

CHARTERS, W.W. (1923) *Curriculum Construction*, New York, US, McMillan.

CHRISTIE, T. and BOYLE, B. (1994a) *Evaluation of Key Stage 3 Assessment: summary report*, Manchester, UK, CFAS/SCAA.

CHRISTIE, T., BOYLE, B. and DEAN, D. (1994b) *Cross Key Stage Comparability in Mathematics'. Intern Report*, Manchester, CFAS/SCAA.

DAVIES I.K. (1976) *Objectives in Curriculum Design*, Narderlead, N'fraw-Hill.

DES (1988) *Report of the Task Group on Assessment and Testing*, London, UK, DES.

GLASER, R. (1963) 'Instructional technology and the measurement of learning outcomes', *American Psychologist*, 18, pp. 519–521.

OFSTED (1993) *Unfinished Business*, London, UK, DES.

SADLER, D.R. (1987) 'Specifying and promulgating achievement standards', *Oxford Review of Education*, **13**, 2, pp. 191–209.

TAYLOR, F.W. (1912) *Scientific Management*, New York, US, Harper.

11 The Relationship of Tests and Teacher Assessment in the Assessment of English at Key Stage 3

Annabel Charles and Andrew Watts

Summary

After the report by Sir Ron Dearing entitled 'The National Curriculum and its Assessment' (1994) the government announced some significant changes to the system of national assessment in England and Wales. This chapter focuses on one of those changes, that is, the requirement for schools to report **both** the teachers' assessments of their pupils and the pupils' results in the national tests. The chapter will principally examine how this change will affect English at Key Stage 3.

Background

In 1988 the Education Reform Act introduced a new National Curriculum and system of national assessment. The report of the Task Group on Assessment and Testing (TGAT) (DES/Welsh Office, 1988), which was used to define the system of assessment, argued that it should be primarily formative, in order not to 'set in opposition the processes of learning, teaching and assessment'. TGAT assumed that the basis of the system would be Teacher Assessment (TA) with standardized assessment tasks (SATs) used to moderate that assessment but not to override it. However the relationship between TA and SATs was never clearly spelt out. The government's formal response to the TGAT report was given in a parliamentary answer (Hansard, 7 June 1988): 'in order to safeguard standards, assessments made by teachers should be compared with the results of the national tests and the judgement of other teachers'. The vagueness of that formulation can no doubt partly be explained by the political opposition that was being expressed to Teacher Assessment. As the system was put into effect its complexity gave additional strength to the arguments against TA and in a series of decisions the government down-played TA's role. By the time the statutory assessment at Key Stage 3 was introduced the assessment still had to result in one reported level for each pupil (on the national ten-level scale), but this level was to be derived for English from the aggregation of the 'standard test' result, with an 80 per cent weighting, and the TA result which had a weighting of only 20 per cent (SEAC, 1992).

Following the boycott of the national tests in 1993 and the Dearing Review, a dual system of reporting was proposed which laid down that the results of the tests and of the TA should be published alongside each other with no aggregation of their results. Some have described this as giving **equal** weighting to the two modes of assessment and have suggested it as a model they would like to replicate at GCSE since it increases the teachers' contribution. However, it would be wrong to see this as equal weighting. What the system does in fact is to leave aside the question of weighting.

This could be seen as a solution to one of the political strains that had been felt in the system. The Dearing Report had removed the need for either side to claim victory for their views. If they wished each could give more credence to the results of their favoured mode of assessment since both were available for inspection. In a speech to the Centre for Policy Studies, in which he was defending his review of the National Curriculum, Dearing said that the dual system of reporting would give parents the opportunity to 'make their own judgements as to the weight to be given to each' (Dearing, 1993). Speaking at the same meeting, but referring to another aspect of the controversy surrounding the review, Lord Skidelsky quoted John Stuart Mill's dictum that 'When experts disagree, let the plain man decide' (Skidelsky, 1993).

Golby (1994) has written that 'Dearing has provided government with expedient political moves, which will in turn have the effect of reopening long-standing debates. Dearing's is a political, not an educational report'. The dual reporting of assessment results could be seen in this light.

Introduction

What benefits are there in a system which acknowledges the differences between modes of assessment by reporting the results of both? We aim to develop the argument that the separate reporting of TA and the test results presents an opportunity to develop a less stressful relationship between the two. Having two modes of assessment standing side by side could emphasize their dissimilarities in a positive way. Each will no longer need to pretend to be doing what the other does better. A tendency for TA to become test-like has been noted by Brown (1991) and Harlen and Qualter (1991), particularly where the purpose is seen to be summative rather than formative. Separating TA and tests could thus positively encourage the different types of information gathering which is advocated as the best practice in TA (BERA Policy Task Group on Assessment, 1992). On the other hand the tests will not have to pretend to cover whole subject domains. The attempt to do this in English at Key Stage 3 led in 1992, for example, to pilot test papers for Literature being set on eleven different set books. It can now be acknowledged that response to literature and wider reading will be covered by the TA rather than the test.

We also discuss the ways in which a dual system of assessment might be perceived by the general public since it is they, and particularly parents, who are now being asked to judge the usefulness of the system. We examine what the users of the system will need to know about the different modes of assessment under the following three headings: the purposes of assessment, the credibility of the dual system and the interpretation of results.

The Purposes of Assessment

We need to start by establishing the different purposes of the two modes of assessment. A distinction that has commonly been made is between 'educational evaluation' and 'managerial evaluation'. Bates says that the former

> . . . assists the teacher to enrich and develop his own teaching [and] can become the basis for educational dialogue with pupils and parents concerning what is being learned and how best to provide various kinds of learning in the future. (Bates, 1984)

The latter is about the grading of pupils and the evaluation of schools' effectiveness. This kind of distinction has also been made by Wood (1986), Troman (1989), Taylor and Wallace (1990) and Gipps (1993). Troman claims that the tension in a system which seeks to combine both purposes for assessment will 'prove intolerable, and will hinder rather than advance the process of education'. The fact that such tensions exist in the present system has been laid at the door of the TGAT report. 'The fundamental mistake that TGAT made — now visible with the benefit of hindsight — was to try to design a single system of National Curriculum Assessment that was simultaneously *formative, summative* and *evaluative* (the last term referring to the Government's requirement that aggregated results for each school be published.)' (Nuttall, 1993).

One of the problems in having a summative purpose for the present assessment system has been that the National Curriculum is criterion based. The two fit uneasily together. In 1986 Harry Black pointed out, on the basis of experience in CSE Mode III, 'If [internal assessment for public examinations] should lead to . . . TA skills in criterion referencing being for summative purposes . . . we will not have capitalized on the substantial potential that criterion-referenced testing has in supporting teaching and learning' (Black H, 1986). Brown described in 1991 the tension that was arising in the new system of TA and SATs because the assessment was supposed to be both formative and summative and she concluded that 'external summative assessment cannot provide reliable results in a criterion-referenced model. . .'. The Dearing Report could therefore be seen as going some way to removing this tension because the basis of the two modes of assessment can now be more clearly

defined, the summative function to be performed by the tests and the formative function by the TA.

Differentiation of Purposes

The BERA Policy Task Group on Assessment (1992) proposed that an assessment system should employ 'different techniques for different assessment
purposes'. The beginnings of such a differentiation are described in SCAA's
School Assessment Arrangements for 1995 booklet for teachers (1994).

> The tests aim to provide a standard, summative 'snapshot' of attain-
> ment at the end of the key stage, based on key aspects of a subject
> which can readily be tested. It is for teacher assessment, undertaken
> in the course of normal teaching and learning, to cover the full range
> of the National Curriculum.

It is noticeable that the purpose of the TA has not been stated here. For 1995
therefore, the link between the tests and the TA will be informal. There has
never been a full system for the auditing or moderation of TA at Key Stage 3
and SCAA is working at present on proposals which could provide for this in
the future. We may, however, reasonably conclude that for the purposes of
teachers, pupils and other internal school audiences, the TA with its informal
process of information gathering over a period of time will be most useful
because of its formative nature. For those wishing to compare the pupils' and
schools' performances with others the tests will be of most interest because of
their greater standardization. The tests will contribute to the standardization of
the TA only insofar as the teachers use them to check the standard of their
own assessments. To see the full picture though, each audience should include in its overall evaluation of the results those produced by **both** modes of
assessment.

Users of the Assessment System

It may be argued that the view expressed above is naive since it will be the
form of assessment that is most obviously summative which will be publicly
more acceptable. However, if we ask which audience for the Key Stage 3 tests
will be most important it seems likely that the answer will be, the parents and
prospective parents of the school. Now the 'free-market' is supposed to be
operating, with schools rewarded financially for persuading parents to send
their children to them, parents have become a more important audience for
schools than, for example, employers. So what is the parents' perception of
the purpose of the tests likely to be?

Parents have not yet had an opportunity to express a view about the assessment system at Key Stage 3, or to contribute to its formal evaluation, but at Key Stage 1 a study by Desforges *et al.* (1994) reported that parents did not have much knowledge of assessment but wanted to know more about it. Parents 'value information about their children's strengths and weaknesses, particularly if this information shows how they can help their children at home'. This suggests that for parents of young children, who do have a view of themselves as partners with the teacher in the child's learning, it is the formative function of assessment which is of most value. It shows that the government correctly identified a desire on the part of parents for more information and involvement. The writers of the above report state however that certain elements of the assessment system, for example the detailed reporting of SAT levels, have been put 'on the market' without having been market tested and their research shows that informing and involving parents is a complex issue, requiring serious consideration of what parents want by both schools and legislators.

At Key Stage 3 the approach of GCSE may affect the parents' perceptions of the purpose of the national tests. TGAT (1988) gave four purposes for the national assessment system: summative, formative, diagnostic and evaluative. Munby (1989) quotes Mackintosh and Hale's six purposes of assessment which divide up the summative function by giving 'prediction', 'grading' and 'selection' separately. The first two of these apply to the assessments at Key Stage 3 and, with GCSE two years away, it could be the predictive function of the Key Stage 3 assessments that will in fact be the parents' main interest. Since prediction implies a measure of planning for further action, parents may well be willing to give at least the same weighting to the formative as to the summative mode of assessment at this stage.

The separate reporting of TA and tests has led to the open recognition that they have different functions. It may also highlight the fact that different users come to the Key Stage 3 assessments for different things. Wiliam (1994b) argues that such issues are sometimes political and not technical and it would be preferable to acknowledge them as such, otherwise 'any kind of meaningful debate is impossible'. Thus the dual system of reporting may prove to be a positive step forward in that it could raise the public awareness about the relationships between the purposes and the processes of assessment.

The Credibility of the Dual System

The word 'credibility' is in the heading above because its lay connotations remind us that the users of the assessments are both professional and non-professional. We could have used the word 'dependability', with its more specialized meaning, which refers to how far the results of an assessment can be assumed to be a representation of a person's overall knowledge and skill in a domain. The dependability, or credibility, of an assessment will depend upon its validity and reliability. Wiliam (1994a) states that 'an assessment is *dependable* to the extent that it is *content valid* and *reliable*'. We therefore need to examine both the National Curriculum tests and the TA in the light of their validity and reliability.

Validity

The validity of tests is not merely a technical matter and, though their focus is limited, they must be credible within the wider context of the curriculum being delivered in schools. Wiliam (1994b) proposes a description of validity that incorporates both the inferences of an assessment and the consequences of it, and he says that these must be seen both within the domain being assessed and beyond it. Such a broad view of validity requires us to take into account teachers' views of the assessment on their teaching, and the public's views on the effects of assessment on children and schools. It is here that the greater explicitness about the coverage of the different modes of assessment will be helpful. What the tests will provide according to SCAA's description above is the evidence of a single, nationally standardized performance that can be taken as typical of the level which a pupil can achieve. The tests will be standardized in the sense that all 14-year-olds will answer the same questions, have the same time and conditions to do them (except those with special exemptions), and have them marked on the basis of the same mark schemes. The tests will be 'based on key aspects of the subject which can readily be tested' (SCAA, 1994 ibid).

The validity of the TA, on the other hand, will be based on its recognition of the complexity and range of the subject. For English, TA will cover the assessment of speaking and listening, which are not tested. It will cover a wide variety of writing tasks which demonstrate the pupils' growing competence in written expression. TA will also look at the pupils' process skills, for example researching, planning and drafting. In their assessments teachers will reflect on the breadth of pupils' reading and the variety of their responses to literature. They will also take into consideration the pupils' involvement in practical work, for example taking part in plays as well as writing about them. Gipps (1993) describes the wide-ranging and informal information gathering that teachers will need to employ if TA is to gather the data which will form the basis of a valid assessment of English. The 'educational' form of assessment she says 'has been introduced to many teachers via the active, process-based SAT tasks. Our hope is that teachers and moderators can build on this experience to become expert observers and assessors of pupils'.

It must be said in this context that the formalization of such assessments, leading as it did to 'excessive workload' complaints, was the reason given for the 1993 boycott of National Curriculum Assessment. Wiliam's definition of validity would require us to consider the impact of assessment on the time available for the delivery of the remainder of the curriculum. In 1993 secondary English teachers were concerned that they would be involved in the same procedures and with as much auditing for TA at Key Stage 3 as they were in preparation for in moderation of pupils' coursework for GCSE. The distinction between the two had not been fully thought through or explained. Therefore the manageability of the assessment and its impact on the time available for teaching are issues which will affect the credibility of the new dual system in the eyes of English teachers.

Reliability

In considering the reliability of an assessment the comparability of results is, according to Pollitt, the key issue. He points out (1994) that comparability year-on-year, between different key stages and between different subjects are three issues which must be tackled in any discussion of the reliability of National Curriculum Assessments (NCA). This arises from the fact that it will be assumed, by the general public at least, that all level 5s, for example, are in some sense equivalent whether they are awarded in Carlisle or Canterbury, in 1995 or 1996, or in English or science. (The need for such results to be interpreted for parents and others is taken up in the following section.) Pollitt concludes that, 'The chief threat to the reliability of the NCA system, in the natural sense of the word, is the failure to ensure that the many tests that report on the same scale are in any sense equivalent'. Since TA is going to report on the same scale it too must, in the criteria it uses to judge performances, be equivalent to the tests, but we would not expect the performances in the two to be necessarily the same. Clearly National Curriculum Assessment is still in its infancy and there is need for research-based development to ensure the production of reliable results from both modes of assessment in the dual system.

Concern about ensuring the reliability of TA has been voiced since the National Curriculum Assessments were introduced. Its supporters have consistently called for in-service training to ensure that the standards for assessment are widely disseminated and understood. Gipps (1994), in commenting on an article by Ann Filer (1994) which describes teacher stereotyping tendencies in TA, writes, 'What we must do, in the name of equity and fairness, is to tie teacher assessment to assessment criteria, provide training in observation and questioning, and offer group moderation to get some consistency, at least, within and across schools'. The BERA Policy Task Group on Assessment (1992) urges that, 'steps be taken to provide teachers with the training and materials so that formative assessment can be carried out with the rigour and reliability necessary for it to be effective in improving pupils' learning . . .' When in July 1994 the government decided to reallocate funds which had been previously allocated for the support of TA, David Hanson, former President of the Association of Assessment Inspectors and Advisers wrote to the *Times Educational Supplement* that this move would 'downgrade the importance of TA . . . The statutory audit of TA is essential if it is to be not only valid but reliable and credible. Equal status between teacher assessment and national tests requires equal rigour'. (Hanson, *TES* July 22nd 1994.) It is clear that for the results of TA to be credible in-service training for it will have to be built into the system.

In all we find that there is cause for concern about the credibility of both the modes of assessment which make up the new system. It will need time for the research and development to be done which will show how effective the system can be. Our concern is that this will inevitably take place in the context of a confrontation based on a simplistic perception that tests mean 'government control' while TA means 'teacher control'. Skidelsky comments that '[the 1993] teachers' revolt over testing which led to the Dearing Review is simply the latest round in the struggle over who "owns" the educational service' (Skidelsky, ibid). We believe that the decision to create a dual system of assessment is a practical way forward which could in time produce credible results.

The Interpretation of Results

A dual system of reporting results will inevitably lead to the demand for satisfactory explanations of the results. Two similar results will not give cause for comment, but when pupils achieve one level in one assessment and another level in the other, the issue of discrepant results will be opened up. It is obvious that many pupils will achieve different levels in two such different modes of assessment. It is difficult to predict how many will be affected. In the following example (Figure 11.1 below) the data relate to an informal survey taken in one county of 1342 pupils from nine schools which had done the 1994 Key Stage 3 English tests (Potter, 1994). Not all the schools had put their results through the official auditing procedure. The results of this survey are given below. In this sample, therefore, more than one quarter of the pupils achieved different levels in the two assessments. Clearly teachers will find they have to explain such differences, not least to parents. It must be acknowledged that this will not merely be synonymous for 'explaining away' the differences.

Levels in English	per cent of pupils
TA same as test level	72
TA 1 level lower than test level	9
TA 1 level higher than test level	17
TA 2 levels lower than test level	0.3
TA 2 levels higher than test level	1.7

Figure 11.1:   One county Key Stage 3 English results (1994)

Levels in English	per cent of pupils in school sample A	B
TA same as test level	87.8	48.0
TA 1 level lower than test level	6.8	3.9
TA 1 level higher than test level	5.4	40.8
TA 2 levels lower than test level	0	0.9
TA 2 levels higher than test level	0	6.4

Figure 11.2: Two school comparison Key Stage 3 English results (1994)

Furthermore, at this early stage in the introduction of the system, it will not be surprising to find significant differences in the results of schools. In Figure 11.2 above, school A in the survey had least differences between TA and test results, and school B had most differences. Clearly the explanation for some of the differences in these figures must be found within individual schools, but that should not be allowed to obscure other factors relevant to the evaluation of the results of individual pupils. In a report written by a head of English department for the Key Stage 3 Project Team on the performance of six pupils in both TA and the 1994 tests, the following reasons were given for differences in some of the assessments of five of the pupils.

> Michael is a good example of a motivated pupil just carried over a level threshold by writing at length, studying with care and a little luck in the marking system.

> Julia's spoken answers in class are often very sharp and show the best side of her English ability. The fact that oral performance will have influenced her TA level is a point to bear in mind.

> I have long seen Emma as at level 6, mostly because her eccentric spelling spoils the surface of her work, and because she is restrained in classroom response . . . In her test I found close answering of the question and useful supporting references (to the play) which made me appreciate that I had underestimated her ability.

> In his anxiety (in the test) to express his extensive knowledge of the play, Jamie had strayed into including what was irrelevant.

> I have tended perhaps to overmark Jenny in my TA because her work is often so beautifully done and because she is so responsive in class.

121

It should be noted that the mark of Jenny in the test was just one below the cut-off of the higher level; an important point since the levels include a wide range of abilities. This indicates the need for parents to be given both the mark from the test and the level which it is said to represent. Overall the explanations above are reasonable and do not cast doubt on either the TA or the test result. It is not surprising that the performances of some pupils were different in two such different assessments. The reporting of both results, with the teacher's comments, gives a fuller picture of the capabilities of the pupils.

Level Descriptions

In the previous section we referred in our comments on the reliability of TA to the need for having agreed criteria on which the assessments will be made. However, one of the strains created by the pre-Dearing National Curriculum Assessment was that it was closely tied to a large number of specific Statements of Attainment. In the new curriculum orders which have emerged as a result of the Dearing Report the attainment criteria have been greatly simplified into level descriptions which could certainly be the basis of both TA and a test specification. Murphy (1994) in describing the limitations of criterion referencing for national assessment welcomes the development of level descriptions: 'These are broader statements, about the typical achievements and attributes of those who are assessed as having reached a particular level, which do not attempt to specify, or guarantee, what each and every pupil at that level can do. This is not, repeat not, criterion-referencing in its purest sense'.

With the dual system of reporting for the National Curriculum Assessment, which will emphasize the different purposes of different assessments, there is an opportunity to be more explicit about the way each mode of assessment relates to the assessment criteria which can be deduced from the National Curriculum level descriptions. In its relation to these criteria the TA element could be described as being criterion referenced. However even in TA the interpretation of the criteria will be dependent on the normative, teachers' judgments that underlie ideas of 'what can be expected of the average child at this age'. The publishing of pupils' graded work for exemplification will promote a common understanding and agreement of the criteria, reinforced by moderation procedures which would involve teachers in matching their interpretation to those of others.

The national tests on the other hand will mainly fulfil a summative function and they will be expected to maintain a standard both geographically and longitudinally. Comparisons will be made between the level 5s given in different counties, in different years, at different key stages and even in different subjects. Pollitt (1994) argues that 'We have in national testing a classic case of a criterion-referenced system that needs normative information in order to set its criteria in a way that will not mislead the public'. Once the standards have been set, pretesting and the use of anchor items to measure the difficulty of each new test will maintain the comparability of results from one year to the next. It would not be possible for such 'normative information' to be explicitly introduced into the TA. Such information can however be built in to the tests and the dual system of assessment gives the opportunity to explain that that is the case.

Conclusion

We have demonstrated that the Dearing solution to the problem of the weighting of teacher assessment and standard tests has been to leave the issue open and let the users of the system decide. This was as much as anything a politically motivated decision, but we have indicated that it does present an opportunity to capitalize on the differences between the two proposed modes of assessment. Research will need to be carried out to tell us how far such a possibility is realized.

We have examined the relationship between the national assessments and those who will use them. We believe that further investigation is needed to understand, firstly, what the different users want from the system and, secondly, what they need to know in order to make best use of the information the system provides. In addition, studies need to be made of the most effective methods of reporting and interpreting results to parents and to other interested members of the public.

We have suggested that one product of such reporting will be more questioning of the processes which underlie both testing and TA. This questioning will take place both among professionals and the public, resulting in the education system being committed to a more open debate about the nature of school assessments. If there is a genuine desire to understand the issues this debate could be helpful. We agree with Wiliam (1994b) that it is better for such questions 'to be addressed explicitly, with the reasons for the solutions adopted being overt, rather than, as is often the case, adopting solutions that are based on implicit, and often covert, assumptions'.

References

BATES, R.J. (1984) 'Educational versus managerial evaluation in schools', *Certification and Control*, London, Falmer Press.
BERA POLICY TASK GROUP (1992) 'Assessment and the improvement of education', *The Curriculum Journal*, **3**, 3, pp. 215–229.
BLACK, H. (1986) 'Assessment for learning', in NATTALL, D. (Ed) *Assessing Educational Achievement*, London, Falmer Press.
BROWN, M. (1991) 'Problematic issues in national assessment', *Cambridge Journal of Education*, **21**, 2, pp. 215–229.
DEARING, R. (1993) 'The review of the National Curriculum and assessment', in LAWLOR,

S. (Ed) *The Dearing Debate. Assessment and The National Curriculum*, Centre for Policy Studies.

DEARING, R. (1994) *The National Curriculum and its Assessment*, SCAA.

DES (1988) *National Curriculum: Task Group on Assessment and Testing: A Report*, London, DES and Welsh Office.

DESFORGES, C., HOLDEN, C. and HUGHES, M. (1994) 'Assessment at Key Stage One: It's effects on parents, teachers and classroom practice', *Research Papers in Education*, **9**, 2, pp. 133–158.

FILER, A. (1994) 'Teacher assessment: A sociological perspective', in HUTCHINSON, D. and SCHAGEN, I. (Eds) *How Reliable is National Curriculum Assessment*? NFER.

GIPPS, C. (1993) *Assessment: A Teacher's Guide to the Issues*, London, Hodder and Stoughton.

GIPPS, C. (1994) 'How reliable is National Curriculum Assessment?' in HUTCHINSON, D. and SCHAGEN, I. (Eds) *How Reliable is National Curriculum Assessment*, Windsor, Berkshire NFER.

GOLBY, M. (1994) 'After Dearing: A critical review of the Dearing Report', *The Curriculum Journal*, **5**, 1, pp. 95–105.

HANSON, D. (1994) 'Letter to' *The Times Educational Supplement*.

HARLEN, W. and QUALTER, A. (1991) 'Issues in SAT development and the practice of teacher assessment', *Cambridge Journal of Education*, **21**, 2, pp. 141–151.

MARTIN, C. (1994) 'Report on the assessment of six pupils in 1994', paper written for UCLES.

MUNBY, S. (1989) *Assessing and Recording Achievement*, Oxford, Blackwell.

MURPHY, R. (1994) 'Dearing: A farewell to criterion-referencing?', *British Journal of Curriculum and Assessment*, **4**, 3, pp. 10–12.

NUTTALL, D. (1993) 'In defence of the TGAT Model', in LAWLOR, S. (Ed) *The Dearing Debate. Assessment and the National Curriculum*, Centre for Policy Studies.

POLLITT, A. (1994) 'Measuring and evaluating reliability in National Curriculum Assessment', in HUTCHINSON, D. and SCHAGEN, I. (Eds) *How Reliable is National Curriculum Assessment*?, Windsor, Berkshire, NFER.

POTTER, S. (1994) 'Circular to heads of English departments in Cheshire schools', *English KS3 Evaluation*, CUPA.

SCAA (1994) 'School Assessment Folder', End of Key Stage Assessment Arrangements for 1995.

SEAC (1992) 'School Assessment Folder', End of Key Stage Assessment Arrangements for 1993.

SKIDELSKY, R. (1993) 'The National Curriculum and assessment: Choice or collectivism', in LAWLOR, S. (Ed) *The Dearing Debate: Assessment and the National Curriculum*, Centre for Policy Studies.

TAYLOR, J. and WALLACE, G. (1990) 'Some dilemmas in implementing the criteria for continuous assessment in GCSE assessment', *British Journal of Sociology of Education*, **11**, 1, pp. 4–65.

TROMAN, G. (1989) 'Testing tensions: The policies of educational assessment', *British Educational Research Journal*, **15**, 3, pp. 279–294.

WILIAM, D. (1994a) 'Reconceptualising validity, dependability and reliability for National Curriculum Assessment', in HUTCHINSON, D. and SCHAGEN, I. (Eds) *How Reliable is National Curriculum Assessment*? Windsor, Berkshire, NFER.

WILIAM, D. (1994b) 'National Curriculum assessments and programmes of study: Validity and impact', Paper presented at a seminar on National Curriculum Testing organized by SCAA, 16 June 1994.

WOOD, R. (1986) 'The agenda for educational measurement', in NUTTALL, D. (Ed) *Assessing Educational Achievement*, London, Falmer Press.

12 Tests, Curriculum and Classroom Practice in Primary Science: Establishing Standards

Terry Russell

Summary

This chapter considers some issues associated with the measurement of standards of performance in science at the end of the primary years, Year 6 (Y6) in England and Wales. Some of the issues discussed are peculiar to primary science but most have implications generalizable to other age groups and subjects once the relationship between the standard tests, the nature of the curriculum, and the manner in which that curriculum is implemented through teachers' classroom practices is taken into account.

Introduction

Whether schools and parents at Key Stage 2 actually share a view of the results of national tests as being of great consequence is not entirely clear. Whatever, it does seem to be the case that expectations as to what the standard tests can produce are often confused and unrealistic. As Black (1993) has pointed out, the tests cannot provide for all three possible assessment outcomes: i) direct assistance to learning in a formative and diagnostic sense; ii) certification of individual pupils; iii) public accountability of institutions and teachers. Elsewhere Black (1994) argues for 'a moratorium on all national assessment for four years', during which time the educationally more critical function of teachers' formative assessment practices (including attention to reliability) would need to be centrally resourced.

> Our present situation is that there is an attempt to serve the Accountability and Certification functions with one set of assessments, while the formative function is undervalued, underdeveloped and confused with teachers' summative assessment. (Black, 1994)

Between 1995 and 2000, there will indeed be a moratorium, but with respect to the curriculum rather than assessment requirements. The standard tests for science at the end of Key Stage 2 carry a burden of responsibility, not to claim to deliver those things that they cannot deliver, but to be consistent with wider educational objectives. The pragmatic line might be to accept the political reality that the tests are likely to continue, and therefore urge that their educational validity be maximized within the constraints which operate. The position adopted here is that the developmental state of primary science education in all its aspects calls for action on all fronts. Best practice (defined as an integration of processes and concepts in teaching and learning) is not widespread; teachers' own science background knowledge remains in need of support; diagnostic assessment is very rarely encountered; teachers doubt the wisdom of teaching some aspects of the prescribed curriculum which in any case has been in flux (major revisions in 1991 and 1994, of what was a novel curriculum in 1988). Summative assessment cannot meet all these needs, but it is suggested that the availability of good summative material could contribute to developments. In the absence of other initiatives, it is understandable that teachers will look to summative assessment to support their interpretation of the curriculum and expectations about standards of performance.

The ideal reform, unlikely to be realized, would be for all three elements — assessment practices, the operationalization and fine-tuning of the curriculum, and teachers' professional development needs — to be receiving continuous attention. A personal view is that the curriculum moratorium should not be five years of suspended animation, but a period of action and reflection during which the curriculum is treated as an hypothesis, the possibilities for its implementation being scrutinized in detail. The system is not of sufficient maturity that summative assessment simply has to solve the technical problems of devising instruments which will provide valid and reliable monitoring of standards in primary science. Much remains to be discovered: about how realistic is the curriculum agenda; about what learning outcomes are possible given optimal support for professional development in the most beneficial teaching and learning environments; and not least, about how assessment opportunities may be of most value to the educational system they inform, within the constraints of the current regime.

Science Curriculum

The backwash effects of summative tests on teachers' practice have long been recognized, but these have tended to be treated as incidental and tacit. Given the state of development of primary science, the test regime has a responsibility to be explicit and accountable for the curricular backwash effects which it generates. There is a danger of a paradoxical and unintended strategy emerging within the rhetoric of raising standards, should summative assessment be suspended until such time as all necessary conditions for delivering the Key Stage 2 science curriculum are in place. That is, standards would not be measured until after they had been raised. The Assessment of Performance

Unit (APU) *Science at Age 11: A Review of Findings* (DES, 1988) reported on the incidence of primary science in England, Wales and Northern Ireland for the years 1980–1984 and concluded:

> Although no recommendation about the proportion of time for science in primary schools was made in 'Science 5–16: A Statement of Policy' (DES, 1985), the figure of 10 per cent for eleven year olds in secondary schools was recognized as appropriate. It would appear inappropriate for eleven year olds in primary or middle schools to have much less than this. The survey findings therefore suggest that two-thirds of schools in England and Wales and four out of five in Northern Ireland fall short of providing adequate time for science activities. (DES, 1988)

Viewed against this baseline, the introduction of science as a mandatory core subject for the 5–11 school population was a revolutionary aspect of the 1988 Education Reform Act (ERA). Of itself it would be expected to have a significant impact on standards, and this would be expected to be a continuing phenomenon as the system geared itself to the new demands. The warnings about backwash have been well-rehearsed over many years: 'teaching to the test' resulting in a narrowing and impoverishment of educational experience are examples of the negative consequences to which educators must be sensitive and alert. The admission of backwash effects may start alarm bells ringing for some, but in the situation in which the tests have a high profile and teachers' subject expertise has far to develop, the backwash effect of the tests has to be not just admitted, but honestly accepted. In fact, it would better be called 'bow-wave' than 'backwash', in recognition of the fact that the national tests are an integral part of the system through which the curriculum is operationalized and standards are defined. As Wiliam (1993) points out, in the classical view, this stance is seen as being the wrong way round, since measurement is concerned with the outcomes of teaching and learning, not *vice versa*.

> An alternative view, that espoused by adherents to measurement-driven instruction (MDI), is that since the test lays out a series of expectations as to what is regarded as important, then in certain circumstances, not teaching to the test would be less in the students' interests than teaching to the test. (Airasian, 1987) (Wiliam, op.cit.)

If this view were to be translated into a mechanical rote training of anticipated test responses, there would be every reason for alarm. More usefully, Airasian's comment serves as a reminder that the relationship between assessment and teaching/learning experiences is multi-faceted. (For example, 'open' examinations, in which candidates have fore-warning of the kinds of questions to which they will be required to respond need not result in a distortion of learning experiences and educationally adverse backwash; they may result in a very positive educational response on the part of students.) Wiliam offers an interesting reformulation for the many types of validity on offer being subsumed under the notion of tests testing something consistent with what teachers might teach (assuming best practice). This is a challenging proposition. It implies that the tests should sample the kinds of behaviours which represent performance in the subject, rather than rote outcomes. Tests that managed to meet this criterion would make the possibility of reviewing summative performance for formative purposes a more realistic possibility, in the sense that they bear a closer correspondence to teaching/learning experiences.

Testing Agenda

The priorities of the School Curriculum and Assessment Authority (SCAA) and its predecessor the School Examination and Assessment Council (SEAC) have been to commission valid and reliable end of key stage standard tests. These tests must be manageable for teachers to administer and to mark. There is a political and a pragmatic imperative to reduce the burden on generalist Key Stage 2 teachers who have all three core subjects to manage. Test administration time is limited and the style of question or test item that may be posed is constrained by considerations about the kinds of marking judgments that markers need to make. The technical constraints on test developers are, as a consequence, severe. The following sections explore some of the issues surrounding attempts to develop summative assessment which is mindful of best practice in Key Stage 2 science, informed where appropriate by evidence drawn from the recently completed NCC-funded project, *Evaluation of the Implementation of Science at KS1–3* (Russell *et al.*, 1994). The author's current experiences with Key Stage 2 standard test development for science in England and Wales also inform some of the issues discussed, but in general terms, rather than specifically related to performance data.

Assessment Implications of Teachers' Science Subject Matter Knowledge

The subject matter of science is unfamiliar to many of those Key Stage 2 teachers who are accountable for its delivery. Teachers are having to teach ideas which may be unfamiliar and regarded as conceptually difficult for their pupils or for themselves. This may result in aspects of the curriculum actually being omitted. The evaluation study found that this was the case for some strands such as the physics content in general (*Energy, Forces, Light and Sound*) as well as *Variation and the Mechanisms of Inheritance and Evolution, (Sc2 strand ii*). The 1994 Dearing Review took some of these matters into account in revising the curriculum.

One consequence of omissions by teachers was that there were clear signs of log-jams building up towards Year 6; pressures to cover the curriculum were consequently exacerbated at the end of the key stage. This in turn led to worries about the coverage of the tests. The four year key stage was assumed by some to imply that there is an enormous volume of 'facts' to be memorized in preparation for assessment at the end of the key stage. Some teachers have suggested that consequently, there is a need for either prior notice of the domains to be tested, ample opportunity for revision or an element of choice for teachers or for pupils. The strategy adopted in test construction has been one of sampling the whole of the Key Stage 2 Programme of Study (PoS) in the tests (sometimes characterized as a fair strategy in being 'equally unfair to all'). Seventy minutes of available test time imposes severe pressures on the achievement of a reliable test. To offer choice, whether to teachers or to pupils, implies the construction of at least a sub-set of test items in parallel form, putting further strains on reliability. Choice might also be seen as compromising the validity of the test, as well as undermining pupils' entitlement, for those conceptual domains which would be avoided are entirely predictable.

Assessment Implications of Teachers' Attitudes Towards Investigatory Science

Although the Non-Statutory Guidance for science suggests that processes and concepts should be seen as 'not in any sense separable' (NCC, 1989), there is little evidence to suggest that this ideal is widespread in Key Stage 2 practice, as yet. The pedagogical knowledge requirements were unfamiliar to some teachers, though Key Stage 2 teachers tend to be positively disposed towards practical or 'hands-on' educational experiences. It happens to be the case that this is precisely the part of the curriculum which is not assessed by the standard tests at the end of Key Stage 2. The SCAA policy has been that anything less than whole investigations in a practical mode would convey the impression that Science Attainment Target 1 (Sc1) could be taught using fragmentary pencil and paper methods. In trying to avoid one kind of wrong impression, inadvertently, another may have been generated — the perception amongst teachers that SCAA is concerned only with pupils' learning of content and concepts, not processes. The fact that teachers are required to assess Sc1 through their Teacher Assessment procedures has not succeeded in countering this interpretation.

More recently, policy has eased on the Sc1 issue, the place of investigatory science in summative assessment. Test development agencies are permitted to set questions within a Sc1 context, with credit being obtained for conceptual application. This makes it possible to present test items which, instead of simply asking for direct recall, ask children to hypothesize about events on the basis of their conceptual understanding or indicate that they are aware (because of their conceptual understanding) of the variables which must be controlled in an investigatory problem. This distinction can be exemplified by two questions which make the same conceptual demand. In version A, the demand is stated directly as concept recall; in version B, the demand is embedded in an investigatory context.

Version A: *M and P are growing some lettuce seeds. What conditions are needed for the plants to grow well?*

Version B: *M and P have two different packets of lettuce seeds. How can they make a fair test to compare how well the two kinds of lettuce plants grow?*

Since question shredding is an apparently irresistible drive in anyone remotely involved with assessment, it is emphasized that the above examples are only outline structures to illustrate a principle. Actual questions would be made more user-friendly with the use of illustrations, for example. The mark schemes would be identical in each case: pupils would be credited for mentioning warmth, moisture, light, possibly a growing medium, etc. Though the logical demand of the two forms is identical, the difference in the presentational format would be predicted to have an impact on performance. In terms of the questions' comparative educational validity, version B would be favoured if it is agreed to be desirable for test items to reflect best pedagogical assumptions or practices. As well as confirming that the knowledge of conditions necessary for plant growth is deemed to be a reasonable expectation in end of Key Stage 2 assessment, the question also carries an implicit message to teachers that such understanding might reasonably be approached through children germinating and growing plants. Though it might be argued that version B is a better example of (or is more consistent with) good practice, in assessment terms it is noteworthy that the question contains twenty-eight words compared with eighteen in version A, with it might be argued consequently greater demands on threshold literacy skills, although the shorter stem (version A) contains the more technical vocabulary 'conditions' to present a contrary argument. Such is item writing!

The national evaluation (Russell, ibid) revealed that teachers had strong ideas about what should be taught and assessed; they had equally strong views about what was inappropriate in the science Order. Some teachers expressed the view that subject matter which could not be taught or made accessible to children via a 'hands-on' approach should not be attempted and should not be part of the Order. These teachers' views might be explained by a firm adherence to stage-developmental notions, specifically, Piaget's descriptions of concrete operational thinking. A particular *bête-noire* was the strand *The Earth's place in the Universe*. If anything was regarded as impossible to address using a 'hands-on' approach, it must be this topic! Some teachers tended to be scathing about direct transmission of knowledge in general. What

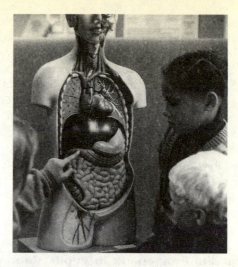

Figure 12.1: KS1 and KS2 science

Figure 12.2: KS1 and KS2 science

seemed to be neglected was a) an admission of the possibility of learning from secondary sources (with echoes of the 1992 Alexander, Rose and Woodhead debate) and b) recourse to the use of concrete models which pupils could manipulate (an issue addressed by Gilbert *et al.*, 1994).

Teachers' scepticism about anything other than 'hands-on' being legitimate experience for Key Stages 1 and 2 science confirmed that careful attention needed to be given to the development of standard assessment items designed to test children's knowledge and understanding of human internal organs, particularly with the idea of supporting good practice. Direct experience seemed an unlikely possibility but three dimensional plaster models offered an excellent substitute. Children were photographed as they dismantled and examined various parts of the model (see Figures 12.1 and 12.2). Various questions about the organs and their functions were combined with the photographs of this exploratory teaching and learning experience.

This was one of the more explicit attempts to illustrate and exemplify good practice through an assessment item. Teachers' feedback to trials of this set of items was not unanimous in its approval. Some teachers indicated that they would seek to make use of models to support children's understanding: the test items would influence their future practice. Some complained that their pupils were unfamiliar with the content of the photographs — the plaster model and its constituent organs — and questioned the validity of the item as a result. Less predictable was the complaint that the photograph of a three-dimensional plaster model of a heart in all its detail did not look like a heart! This may be a strong case of epistemological relativity: what hearts really look like depends on your purpose in observing them.

Assessment and Progression in Pupils' Conceptual Understanding

Within current constructivist thinking in science education (see for example, Pfundt and Duit, 1994; Black and Lucas, 1994) progression in the complexity and quality of children's understanding of scientific ideas is regarded as important. That pupils' understanding progresses is by no means regarded as axiomatic by primary teachers. Long ago, in my early days as a primary teacher, progression in my inexperienced teaching of mathematics was ensured by the fact that page two in the pupils' books always followed page one. This made me feel secure until I had achieved a better grasp of teaching mathematics and I can empathize with similar strategies being sought by teachers of primary science (supported by National Curriculum ring-binders). Possibly as the result of a lack of familiarity with the major ideas of science on the part of some teachers, science learning may be treated as the acquisition of a mass of unrelated facts. Though not necessarily the majority position, a significant number of teachers seem to hold this atomistic view. There are dangers associated with assessment which ignores progression. Criterion-referenced assessment which generates dichotomous outcomes ('criterion met' or 'criterion not met') may unintentionally reinforce the idea that the assessment regime is designed to find out whether discrete facts are known or not known. Successful diagnostic assessment implies that teachers are able to locate children's ideas on some kind of developmental pathway; such knowledge informs the tailoring of appropriate teaching and learning experiences. Summative assessment items should, at the very least, be capable of being mapped onto the same developmental sequences, even though the purposes for which the results are generated may be different. There should be a common and recognizable agenda of progression in pupil understanding shared by summative and formative tests, even if the diagnostic instruments and practices are not widespread currently.

(N = 519 KS1 and KS2 teachers, per cent)					
	Very Confident			**Not Confident at all**	
	1	**2**	**3**	**4**	**5**
English (n = 508)	24	51	21	3	–
Mathematics (n = 507)	19	55	23	3	–
Science (n = 506)	5	36	47	11	1

Figure 12.3: KS1–2 teachers' understanding of children's development in core subjects

The evaluation study (Russell, ibid) included a questionnaire probe of teachers' confidence in knowing how children's understanding develops in each of the three core subjects. The response rate from teachers of Key Stages 1 and 2 was 59 per cent, giving 519 responses as summarized in Figure 12.3. A rating of 1 represented 'very confident'; 5 represented 'not confident at all'. The mean rating for English was 2.0; for mathematics it was 2.1; science trailed behind the other two core subjects with a mean rating of 2.7. Only 40 per cent of the teachers indicated feeling 'confident' or 'very confident' about knowing how children's understanding develops in science, while the equivalent proportion for English was 75 per cent and for mathematics 74 per cent. Ideas of progression in the development of children's understanding have to be incorporated in the assessment programme. If this is achieved, summative tests can also yield information of formative value. An example drawing on the assessment of a Statement of Attainment (SoA) from the 1991 version of the science curriculum will illustrate this point more clearly:

AT4 strand(v) statement 2e: know that the Earth, Sun and Moon are separate spherical bodies

It would be all too easy in testing this SoA to offer pupils a multi-choice array of geometric shapes — cube, cone, pyramid, sphere, disc etc. and then to ask them to select the one that matches the shape of the Earth, Moon, or whatever. But this is an impoverished approach for at least three reasons:

The question does not incorporate or imply good practice. Can we envisage a primary teacher enacting such an activity?

The question invites only a right or a wrong response, and the wrong responses yield no insights into the manner in which children have arrived at their response decision. (This is not a requirement of a summative test item, but should a teacher choose to review children's test performance for diagnostic insights into what children know and where they might be experiencing difficulties, it should be capable of providing such information.)

Most importantly, the item does not tap understanding capable of being located at some point on the known developmental pathway of children's understanding of the Earth as a spherical body.

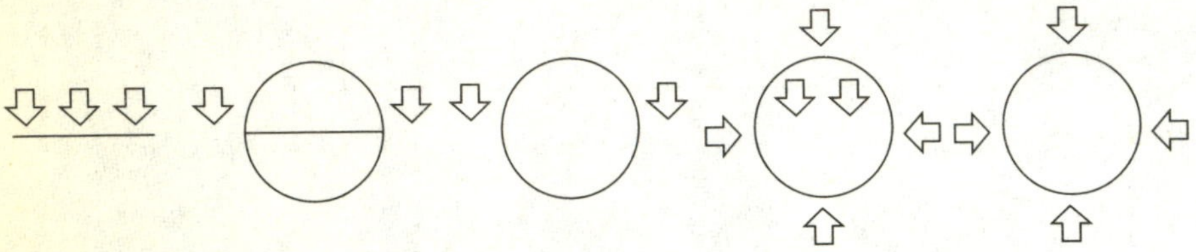

Five notions of the Earth as a cosmic body. (Nussbaum and Sharoni-Dagan, 1983)

Figure 12.4:   Examples of children's progress in understanding in science

Research which describes the progression in children's ideas is available, though nobody would claim that it is complete. Figure 12.4 summarizes in schematic form the progression in children's ideas which research has identified. (There are many more such examples of progression in the research literature. This example has been selected because it is compact, quickly communicable and represents an area of the curriculum which caused some pedagogical concerns.)

The arrows in the diagram represent children's assumptions about the direction of the action of the force of gravity. The first idea is of a 'flat-Earth'; the next three show that an appreciation of the Earth as a sphere may carry strongly egocentric ideas about what is 'down'. Only in the fifth example is there an appreciation that the Earth is a sphere that people can live all around, with 'down' being relative. This is no longer a trivial understanding in the way that mere matching of shapes is; it is clear that an idea that the Earth is shaped like a ball can be maintained alongside ideas profoundly at odds with the location of 'up' and 'down'.

Progression in the National Curriculum

It has been argued above that there is an essential inter-relatedness between the curriculum, what is assessed, and teaching and learning experiences in the classroom. Each component must refer to and be informed by the other two. With the curriculum in flux and primary teachers' professional development in continuing need of support, there is imbalance and asymmetry in this inter-relatedness. Key Stage 2 assessment cannot point to years of precedent in good science practice and established standards of performance. In the absence of such bench-marks, test developers must turn to research evidence as an alternative touchstone. Fortunately, there is a considerable volume of relevant research (Pfundt and Duit, 1994), though relatively little has percolated through to influence primary practice as yet.

Progression has been a concern to the authors of the National Curriculum. A major component of the NCC funded evaluation programme (Russell, ibid) was a study on Progression. The NCC specification for the national evaluation project stated the following:

> There are problems with the level of difficulty of some Statements of Attainment. Evaluation will identify further examples of inappropriate levels and progression and make recommendations for amendment.

The study used interview and questionnaire techniques followed by in-depth work with groups of teachers representing Key Stage 1, 2 and 3. The researchers visited classrooms, observed teaching and learning activities and talked to both teachers and pupils. Diagnostic assessment activities were developed. Pupils were also interviewed to establish their understanding of the concepts under consideration. All of these activities served to clarify for the participating teachers and for the collaborating researchers, what the conceptual domain meant in operational form, and what was possible or realistic to attempt to teach to children of various ages. The cross-phase fertilization was enormously valuable. The meetings were much more focused and mutually productive than has often been the case with traditional cross-phase continuity meetings.

As the result of the activities described above, detailed recommendations were made to SCAA about smoothing the progression in the strands which had been researched. It was also pointed out that further collaborative research with teachers would be invaluable. The specific findings are presented elsewhere (Russell *et al.*, 1994, Vol 2). It is the mechanism that is of interest in the present context of attempts to set standards. Insights into ideas of progression were especially valuable; progression was defined by reference to three interacting elements: the curriculum (PoS and SoA) as an agenda for teaching and learning; the operational programme of teaching and learning experiences generated by teachers on the basis of that curriculum; the cognitive capabilities and limits of progression in knowledge and understanding of pupils studying within the guidelines of the curriculum.

Too often, teachers are left out of considerations about progression. It is they who interpret, operationalize and implement the curriculum. It is they who enable pupils to achieve certain understandings. It is teachers who mediate the transmission of the sub-set of cultural knowledge with which science education is concerned. One of the problems associated with attempts to reflect progression in Key Stage 2 summative tests was that, despite the large number of Statements of Attainment, the 'Strands of Progression' in the curriculum were incomplete. Another problem is that research into progression in understanding in all conceptual domains is also incomplete. In the 1994 revision of the curriculum, Statements of Attainment have been replaced by Level Descriptions. These Level Descriptions are intended to encourage teachers to make more holistic and synoptic end of Key Stage assessment judgments. Though they do include some domain-specific illustrations of learning outcomes, the Level Descriptions necessarily verge towards being an information-processing (i.e. content free) hierarchy. ('Necessarily' because the levels are abstractions across a range of diverse subject-matter.)

One of the implications of the more general Level Descriptions is that, in combination with the content prescribed in the programmes of study, novel pairings can be generated. This opens up the possibility of writing test items which meet the demands of different Level Descriptions within a domain, and in doing so, reveal an implicit progression. For example, test items about light could be written to every level; the fact that learning outcomes are not specified for every domain is not a hindrance, but a liberty, to a test development agency.

It must also be appreciated that the change to Level Descriptions is a paradigm shift in moving from a domain-specific notion towards information-processing assumptions about progression. Concept development research tends to suggest that progression in different domains does not follow parallel or equivalent paths. There is a reminder here of the dissatisfactions with Piaget's stage developmental model being shored up with notions of vertical and horizontal 'decalages' to explain away differences in individuals' cognitive-developmental levels across a range of subject matter. Some will no doubt be drawn to an exploration of the construct validity of the hierarchy of Level Descriptions. The Level Description scale is more likely to be useful simply as an enabling device against which to peg domain specific progression in science performance.

The Need to Develop Diagnostic and Formative Teacher Assessment

Though the summative functions of assessment have dominated debate, Dearing has stressed the limited function of the summative tests: 'formal end of key stage testing has so far played only a modest part in the assessment of the National Curriculum' (Dearing, 1993, para 5.8). This may seem suspiciously like casting a veil of understatement over most people's perception; the position is justified by the recognition of the accompanying and complementary role of 'sensitive and thorough diagnostic and formative teacher assessment' (Dearing, op.cit. p. 48). This is a laudable sentiment; elsewhere it has been suggested that this teacher assessment will not only be complementary but will be endowed with 'parity of esteem'. The reality, at least as far as Key Stage 2 science is concerned, is that, though the rhetoric suggests that it will be warmly welcomed when it appears on the scene, 'sensitive and thorough diagnostic and formative teacher assessment' is only sporadically visible on the horizon. This is simply a developmental fact. Just as the science curriculum is still being invented (and re-invented) and just as summative assessment structures are still being defined, formative assessment is still on the drawing boards. There are familiar reasons and recent evidence as to why this is the case.

Science Interview:			
'While you are teaching, how do you find out whether pupils are learning?'			
	KS1 **(n = 29)**	**KS2** **(n = 51)**	**KS3** **(n = 42)**
Talking to pupils	66	57	64
Observing pupils talking together	55	45	52
Written work	17	45	57
Question and Answer	24	31	52
Class discussion	3	6	21
Tests	10	18	50
Children applying one task to another situation	10	12	7
Watching pupils' reactions	–	–	12
Teacher experience	10	–	–
Teacher instinct/intuition	–	6	2

Figure 12.5: Teachers' formative assessment methods

In the course of the NCC evaluation programme, comments were invited from teachers as to the methods they used to monitor pupils' learning. Data were collected from a national interview sample by asking the question: 'While you are teaching, how do you find out whether your pupils are learning?' (see Figure 12.5). Talking to pupils was the most frequently used strategy at all key stages (66 per cent Key Stage 1; 57 per cent Key Stage 2; 64 per cent Key Stage 3). Observing pupils talking together was also frequently used (55 per cent Key Stage 1; 45 per cent Key Stage 2; 52 per cent Key Stage 3). These are both very direct methods, in contrast to the written format of the summative standard tests. Tests and other forms of written assessment become more prevalent as children move into Key Stage 3: teachers appear to deem 'tests' more appropriate at Key Stage 3; at this point, writing skills will be less of a hurdle to pencil and paper assessment of science.

Most of these responses are analytical in nature, but it is interesting that a minority responded in a non-operational manner using terms such as 'intuition', 'instinct' or 'experience'. What seemed to be lacking was any purposely constructed direct methods which could be used to probe children's understanding pro-actively.

Conclusion

Formative and diagnostic teacher assessment is sorely in need of support, a major reason being the political pre-occupation with summative measures. Teachers need specific support in developing experience of the progression of ideas. Summative assessment, being a conspicuous aspect of every teacher's professional life, could begin to build bridges in that direction. Therefore, the decision to contract test marking to outside agencies is a regrettable erosion of opportunities for teachers to gain direct feedback about different qualities of pupil performance.

The objective of measuring changes in standards of achievement of pupils in science in England using valid and reliable seventy minute standard tests of a common curricular experience is a challenging undertaking. Many of the critical variables remain in flux: teachers' subject and pedagogical knowledge, the assessment structure, the curriculum itself.

Standards of Key Stage 2 science have no doubt been raised subsequent to the ERA, by virtue of the fact that the subject has become a mandatory core subject — not as the result of performance being measured. However, assessment has played a role in helping to operationalize the curriculum. The relationship between curriculum, assessment and teaching and learning practices in the classroom must be treated as inter-related and interactive. Summative assessment must be sensitive to pedagogical implications.

If the positivist goal were to be relaxed, the Key Stage 2 science curriculum could be thought of as an hypothesis about what might be taught and what understanding might be achieved by pupils. The summative assessment programme can provide unparalled feedback of an iterative and cumulative kind about pupil performance following known curricular experiences. This is an advocacy of assessment as a component of a broader programme comprising a curriculum development exercise informed by performance data. We remain far removed from such a research-based assessment strategy. The current proposal for Level Descriptions represents a paradigm shift from a conceptually based scale to one which is process-based. The debate about standards is understandably influenced by thinking about normative procedures, including those which invite teachers' judgments. There is a case which can be made for alternatives to approaches derived from consensus, looking instead at teachers' optimal practices. This approach acknowledges teachers' roles in any consideration of pupil progression in understanding.

References

AIRASIAN, P. (1988) 'Measurement-driven instruction: A closer look', *Educational Measurement: Issues and Practice*, (Winter) pp. 6–11.

ALEXANDER, R., ROSE, J. and WOODHEAD, C. (1992) 'Curriculum organisation and classroom practice in primary schools', A Discussion Paper, London, DES.

BLACK, P.J. (1993) 'Formative and summative assessment by teachers', *Studies in Science Education*, **21**, pp. 49–97.

BLACK, P.J. (1994) 'Alternative education policies: Assessment and testing', in TOMLINSON, S. (Ed) *Educational Reform and Its Consequences*, London, IPPR/Rivers Oram Press, Chapter 8.

BLACK, P.J. and LUCAS, A.M. (Eds) (1993) *Children's Informal Ideas in Science*, London, Routledge.

DEARING, R. (1993) *The National Curriculum and its Assessment*, Interim Report, NCC and SEAC, July 1993.

DES (1985) *Science 5–16: A Statement of Policy*, London, HMSO.

DES (1988) *Science at Age 11. A Review of APU Survey Findings 1980–84*, Department of Education and Science. Welsh Office, Department of Education for Northern Ireland, Her Majesty's Stationery Office.

GILBERT, J., BRODIE, T., HOLLINS, M., RAPER, G., WEBB, M. and WILLIAMS, J. (1994) *Models and Modelling in Science Education*, Association for Science Education.

NCC (1989) *Science Non-Statutory Guidance*, York, National Curriculum Council.

NUSSBAUM, J. and SHARONI-DAGAN, N. (1983) 'Changes in second grade children's preconceptions about the Earth as a cosmic body resulting from a short series of audio-tutorial lessons', *Science Education*, **67**, pp. 99–114.

PFUNDT, H. and DUIT, R. (1994) *Bibliography: Students' Alternative Frameworks and Science Education*, 4th Edition. Kiel, IPN.

RUSSELL, T., QUALTER, A. and McGUIGAN, L. (1994) *Evaluation of the Implementation of Science in the National Curriculum*, Volumes 1, 2 and 3, School Curriculum and Assessment Authority.

WILIAM, D. (1993) 'Reconceptualising validity, dependability and reliability for National Curriculum assessment', Paper for symposium on *Investigating Variability on National Curriculum Assessment*, British Educational Research association, Liverpool, September.

13   Mark Schemes and Levels of Thinking in Geography

Peter Davies

Summary

Marks awarded in secondary school geography through public examinations
have become associated with descriptions of attainment. This association has
developed over time through custom and practice as well as by the influence
of criteria published by examination bodies and authorities. These published
criteria have influenced practice through encouraging emphases in marking
even when cast in very general terms. The reasoning behind such generality
being that more detailed criteria reduce teachers' and examiners' room for
manoeuvre. However, it is apparent from analysis of scripts and mark schemes
that the relationship between marks awarded and level of attainment is largely
in the hands of the examiner. This chapter examines how that influence is
wielded in geography. The focus of attention is the design of mark schemes
for questions which allow a variety of creditable responses. If we give four
marks for one answer to a question and two marks for another answer to the
same question, what is it that differentiates the weight of marks between these
answers?

Differentiation Through Point Marking Schemes

Although they have not usually been designed as such, point marking schemes
embody a form of differentiation by outcome. Pupils who have been asked to
describe the distribution of an industry or to explain its decline are differentiated on the basis of how many points of description or explanation they can
offer. This method can be defended on the grounds that higher levels of
achievement in geography are demonstrated through greater breadth of observation and a recognition of multiple causes. It can be criticized on the grounds
that it frequently differentiates on the basis of recalled descriptions and reasons which do not embody any transferable characteristics of describing or
reasoning in geography. An example of a mark scheme and two sample pupil
responses to a GCSE question are shown in Figure 13.1. The relevant question

140

Question: Give **Two** reasons for the changes in the amount of coal used.

Mark scheme:
Any **two** of: stocks running out / geological difficulties / too expensive / end of steam trains / dirty / oil and gas fired central heating / other fuels / harmful to environment etc.
1 point for each correct response. Total 2 marks.

Pupil A: 'Because coal has become more expensive and the seams that are left are more difficult to mine.'
Pupil B: 'Because the seams that are left are more difficult to mine and *this has made* coal more expensive.'

Figure 13.1:   GCSE point mark scheme

stem is also included as a point of reference. The explanations in the mark scheme are specific to the coal industry. They do not distinguish in levels of achievement between Pupil A whose answer suggests that he/she has learnt these reasons as **points to recall** and Pupil B who is able to **relate the points** in his/her explanation. This example illustrates the case that in addition to ignoring lines of reasoning, a point-form mark scheme is not suited to handling probabilities or consistency with evidence. Has the depletion of reserves exerted a significant effect on the level of coal production in the United Kingdom (UK)? These problems are still there if the question invites pupils to make use of stimulus data. For instance, suppose the question provides the following data: change in the level of total coal production in the UK, change in the level of estimated reserves of coal, change in the price of coal, and a short piece of text in which a source argues that pits must be closed because too much coal is being produced, and pupils are asked to 'Use the data and your own knowledge to explain why coal production is falling in the UK'. A point form mark scheme encourages a pupil to list in isolation separate points of explanation from the data (on a comprehension of statistics and text basis) and add points of their own to the list.

Differentiation Through Levels of Response

An analysis of GCSE papers from one examination board (Figure 13.2) suggests that 'point-form' marking still dominates examination marking in geography for 16 year olds. However, these papers also use 'levels of response' mark schemes which characteristically divide responses into three categories: low, medium or high. The categorization of responses in this manner suggests that each level of response possesses a distinctive characteristic which goes beyond the simple accumulation of points. Do these characteristics exist and, if so, what are they? The analysis in Figure 13.2 suggests a small number of frequently recurring criteria which are used to distinguish higher levels of response. These are (i) greater specificity; (ii) adding a link to a small chain of variables; and (iii) recognizing conflicting points of view. Greater specificity is sometimes sought in the application of general themes to the characteristics

Basis for differentiation: Marks awarded by level of response								
Syllabus	(1)	(2)	(3)	(4)	(5)	(6)	(7)	(8)
A*	48	9	0	0	14	27	2	0
B	66	7	5	10	2	8	2	0
C	75	0	0	0	0	20	3	2
D	76	3	0	2	1	13	3	2
E	63	11	10	0	0	8	2	6

* The only one of the syllabuses to include a multiple choice paper. Marks for this paper are excluded.

Key to figure: (1) = Points made   (5) = Parts/Whole

(2) = Number of points   (6) = Specificity

(3) = Elaboration   (7) = Context

(4) = Describe/Explain   (8) = Balance

Figure 13.2: *Proportion of marks awarded in GCSE geography mark schemes*

of particular places, but frequently it is sought in the detail associated with more specific knowledge of a stereotype (e.g. 'the benefits and problems of tourism in rural areas'). An example of 'adding a link to a small chain of variables' in a description of a 'high level response' in a mark scheme is found in a question in which pupils are asked to explain how some climate data affects the suitability of a region for farming. At a 'mid' level pupils are expected to match a characteristic of the climate ('mild winters') with a type of farming ('dairy farming') whilst a high level response is expected to refer to 'how' this link is made (i.e. 'through helping the growth of pasture'). An example of recognizing conflicting points of view is to be found in a mark scheme which describes a 'high level response' as mentioning 'good points and bad' of tourism in rural areas. The GCSE mark schemes reviewed in Figure 13.2 use 'specificity' as the major basis for distinguishing higher from lower levels of response.

One justification for a level of response mark scheme is that it allows some credit to be given to pupils who are 'working towards' a satisfactory response whilst also providing an opportunity to recognize 'progress beyond a satisfactory level'. Another justification is that by describing characteristics of levels of response attention is focused on the quality of thinking displayed in the answer, in which recalled knowledge is used rather than regurgitated. However, 'levels of response' mark schemes are open to criticism. The standardized use of three categories 'high', 'medium' and 'low' suggests that the classifications are always imposed rather than arising from the kinds of difference which might be expected in answers to a given type of question. Why not sometimes two or four levels of response categories? In addition, there is a tendency for levels to be distinguished by phrases such as 'vague response', 'ideas developed in more detail', and 'deals with processes more thoroughly' which are qualitatively unspecific and leave the basis for differentiation unclear. There is an obvious danger, in these circumstances, that differentiation will occur on the basis of pupils' linguistic rather than geographical ability, not least in how much they write, a quantitative rather then qualitative response measure.

On this analysis of custom and practice in geography GCSE examinations there are evidenced characteristics of better answers which reflect higher levels of subject specific attainment. However, these characteristics are used on a rather haphazard basis even within the same examination paper. This failure to utilize a potentially useful measurement device may be encouraged by the focus in mark scheme writing on desired responses rather than the demonstration of desired levels of attainment. This, in turn, may be related to a too rigid adherence to the methodology of a set format of 'high', 'medium' and 'low' responses with the resultant temptation to describe appropriate responses in a general, non-subject specific form (e.g. 'vague response'). Greater clarity in illustrating and exemplifying desired levels of attainment may help to produce mark schemes which are more subject focused whilst discouraging the accumulation of marks simply on the basis of recalled descriptions and explanations. The second half of the chapter analyzes pupils' responses to test questions in the search for characteristic types of thinking on which 'desired levels of attainment' might be based.

Differentiation in the National Curriculum Key Stage 3 Pre-tests and National Pilot

During the pre-testing and national pilot stages of the development of tests for Key Stage 3 in the National Curriculum by the Centre for Formative Assessment Studies, University of Manchester during 1992 and 1993 (Christie *et al.*, 1993) pupils' answers were analyzed for differences in response. While the tests themselves and the statements of attainment they referred to are, post-Dearing, consigned to the water under the bridge category of development, some evidence from this analysis can be used to consider levels of response in geography. This analysis is exploratory and some results are presented here principally to encourage further investigation. The analysis has taken two forms: (i) categorizing different types of response and (ii) investigating the association between types of response to different questions.

The categorization of responses is undertaken in the search for types of thinking that are revealed by the answer, rather than styles of response which are dictated by the peculiarities of the question. This is obviously a developmental and potentially subjective exercise, hence the need for further investigation. There is a danger that differences will exist only in the eye of the onlooker and that those differences are created by the form of the question. Some checks and balances may be built in by individuals independently scrutinizing responses and drawing up their own classifications, but ultimately mutual agreement will be necessary to determine which differences really matter. The applicability of the same classification to responses for different questions also begins to extend the confidence in the findings. One inescapable issue is that experience of marking pupils' exam scripts indicates that pupils' written answers in tests will be heavily influenced by their beliefs about what the examiner wants and how these expectations have been trained by their teachers. It may well be that types of thinking revealed under these circumstances bear no relation to the pupils' thinking when confronted by similar questions and issues in other contexts, particularly in their everyday experience. Evidence on this problem in geography has yet to be gathered, but the experience of other subjects (e.g. Driver, 1983; Lave, 1992) suggests it is immense. Nevertheless, as long as we rely chiefly on written assessments and examinations we will have to find ways of making the best of a problematic job.

Some differences between pupils' answers to test questions are summarized in the following section. The differences have been grouped under three main headings: A: specificity, B: contextualization, and C: viewpoints and perceptions which have some correspondence with characteristics which have been used to distinguish answers in levels of response mark schemes.

Specificity refers to the acuity with which pupils recognize the particular in places. At lower levels, progress is seen primarily in the use of more discriminating classifications with increasing accuracy. At higher levels a prime aspect of 'specificity' is the recognition of the interaction of a combination of characteristics in creating the nature of a place. *Contextualization* refers to a pupil's ability to set observations, events and decisions within increasingly complex frameworks. This increase in complexity is evident in (i) the way that pupils handle time in their explanations; (ii) the realism of pupils' portrayal of motivation and the degree of freedom enjoyed by different individuals and organizations; (iii) pupils' recognition of interdependence between places; and (iv) the sophistication of their modelling in terms of number of variables and the type of relationship between variables. *Viewpoints and perceptions* refer to a pupil's ability to move beyond stereotypical labelling of places and activities, a one sided perception of issues and the treating of conflicts of interest as simply a battle between roles to judgments which are more cautious in the face of the diversity of places and perceptions. Verbatim extracts from pupils' answers to illustrate the differences in thinking implied in responses follow.

A: Specificity

Between levels 2 and 4

From using a single descriptor (very hilly) to a classification of features (e.g. lowland, coast and mountain) when describing a locality or region.

From recognizing a criterion (e.g. width of river, type of housing) to using the criterion accurately (e.g. narrow channel, semi-detached) when describing features.

Between levels 3 and 5

From recognizing a process or set of events (e.g. 'wearing away', 'weather' or 'using things up') to using sub-categories (e.g. climate/weather, erosion/weathering; renewable/non-renewable) when making sense of changes in the human and physical environment.

From accounts of events (e.g. effects of an increase in traffic or an example of water pollution) which are stereotypical (e.g. 'Tourist attractions, hotels etc. have dumped their wastes in the sea') to accounts which give some sense of 'how' and 'where' (e.g. 'oil was spilt into the Pacific Ocean and left for three days when there was a storm which spread the oil further').

Between levels 4 and 6

From linking a process with a feature (e.g. 'more visitors' with 'worn foot-paths'; 'erosion by waves' with 'cliffs') to linking a process with a characteristic of a feature (e.g. 'more visitors' with 'wider and muddier footpaths'; 'erosion by waves' and 'undercutting of cliffs').

Between levels 4 and 7

From explanations of events (e.g. soil erosion) which give one acceptable indication of either 'how' or 'where' (e.g. 'When it rains soil is picked up with water, taking it away') through handling both 'how and where' (e.g. 'Deforestation of the slopes of the Himalayas leads to it') to an explanation in which two or more features of a place are combined *in sequence* (e.g. 'In the tropical rainforests humans cut down trees and farm the land, then leave it. The soil has no nutrients or anything to hold it so it just washes away').

From accounts of a sequence of events (e.g. convectional rainfall) which refer to a couple of steps in a sequence (e.g. 'evaporates then it rains') to accounts which refer to several steps and give some indication of what is prompting the sequence (e.g. 'Because it was hot during the day the sea warmed up causing more water to evaporate. The warm air rose and got cooler and you got more condensed so the clouds had to let it out').

B: Contextualization

Between levels 3 and 5

From explanations of human activity (e.g. locating economic activity; polluting) which refer only to the location of the activity (e.g. 'This would be a good site for a superstore because it is next to a main road') to explanations which link the activity with other places (e.g. 'It's a good place for a factory because it is near a main road so you can export the produce').

From explanations of human activity (e.g. why motorways tend to go round rather than through cities, what attracts people to go to live in a place) which limit motivation to their own, young person orientated perspective (e.g. 'It's too dangerous' *to have a motorway in a city*; 'It's got a camp site and museums to visit') to explanations which reflect the influence of different roles, cultures and circumstances on motivation (e.g. 'They — *motorways* — bypass them to help traffic round instead of through', 'They might get a job in the shops or offices in the town').

Between levels 4 and 6

From linking a distribution (e.g. of volcanoes, of flooding) or change (e.g. in size of population) with one variable (e.g. 'You find volcanoes at the edge of plates'; 'the population goes up if families have more children') to treating a distribution or change as contingent on a couple of variables (e.g. 'Population will go up if more babies are born in a year than you have people dying').

From identifying likely effects of an event (e.g. an earthquake or the building of a new facility) without a sense of time scale (e.g. either referring to the effects of building a new car park for visitors in a rural area in terms of 'cutting down trees to make way' or referring only to 'more cars visiting the area causing pollution') to identifying likely effects in the context of a time scale (e.g. referring to an immediate effect and a later effect).

Between levels 5 and 8

From treating the relationship between two variables as singular (e.g. 'Countries with higher standards of living use more energy') to recognizing plurality in relationships (e.g. 'Although people in richer countries usually use more energy, countries with lots of energy tend to be more wasteful') due to the combinations of circumstance faced in different places.

From treating environmental problems (e.g. pollution, flooding, desertification) as the outcomes of accidents, attitudes or poverty (e.g. 'The sea was polluted with oil because the tanker hit some rocks'; 'The Mediterranean is polluted because all the hotels just pour their rubbish into the sea', 'The people in Bangladesh get flooded as they haven't got enough money to move somewhere else') to treating these problems as the outcomes of connecting circumstances (e.g. *explaining desertification*, 'If a group of people settle they overwork the soil around them, growing the same types of crops and giving the soil no time to regain its nutrients. Also, when they cut down native trees for firewood the soil is no longer bound together by roots and it becomes dry. When there is a drought, people take more water for themselves to survive and leave little for the plants').

From recognizing both short and long-term effects of an event to recognizing factors affecting the pace and scale of change including the way in which short term changes lead to other longer term changes (this is exemplified in the desertification answer quoted above and explanations of 'knock-on' or 'multiplier' effects in industrial change).

From setting an event or distribution of features (e.g. the location of superstores in an urban area) in one context (e.g. only in terms of accessibility to consumers, location decisions made by producers, the planning policy of local or national government or a trend in the concentration of retailing) to an ability to recognize and handle some implications of more than one of these contexts.

C: Viewpoints and perceptions

Between levels 4 and 7

From recognizing one perception of an environmental issue (e.g. the potential of jobs created by a quarry or the noise created by additional quarry traffic) to recognizing more than one perception of the issue.

From treating a conflict of interest as a battle between roles (e.g. farmers versus walkers) to recognizing the focus of conflict (e.g. cars blocking gateways) which may, or may not be capable of resolution (e.g. through car parks).

From labelling activities as 'good' or 'bad' and places as 'problems' (e.g. 'oil and gas cause pollution, but H.E.P has no effect'; 'Africa is overpopulated') to basing judgments on evidence of characteristics of activities or places.

Differences within these three broad areas of progression are allocated to a range of levels rather than to specific levels. This is due to the caution which is needed in interpreting the data generated through the process of pre- and pilot testing in the development of Key Stage 3 tests. The imperative of issuing definitive documents for the National Curriculum has pushed the allocation of particular achievements to specific levels ahead of the evidence needed to justify such actions, and there is no indication in present events that this tendency has abated.

It is also important to remember that a consistent quality of difference may be observed in the answers of a group of pupils to questions on diverse

Question summary	Answer of pupil A	Answer of pupil B
1 Required two reasons why the location shown on the map provided would be good for an economic activity suggested by the pupil	Near a main road so you can export Plenty of houses for employees to live in	Near a busy main road Villages and towns nearby
2 Required pupils to name an economic activity and place of location they had studied and explain why the location was a good one	Farming in England — correct climate for crops	Tourist industry in Italy — hot beach resort, historical place which offers a lot for tourists
3 Required pupils to explain the cause of an example of water pollution in a named place they had chosen	Due to huge tourist industry, the country could not cope with the sewage so they dumped it in the sea	Because the farmer allowed the pesticides to drain from the land into the river

Figure 13.3: *Answers of two pairs of pupils to questions*

themes without this consistency appearing in the answers of individual pupils. For example the answers of two pupils to three different questions are shown in Figure 13.3. Would you judge the thinking of these pupils to be at the same or different levels? Pupil A consistently sets answers in a richer — in this case economic — context (by referring to 'so you can export', 'for employees to live in' and 'Due to huge tourist industry, the country could not cope with the sewage'). These answers suggest at least a level 5 response as links with other places are recognized and an environmental problem is presented as an outcome of circumstances. However, pupil B is consistently more specific ('near a busy main road', 'hot beach resort, historical place which offers . . .', 'allowed pesticides to drain from land into the river'). This attention to 'how and where' suggests level 5. One pupil demonstrates one broad characteristic of 'better explanation', whilst the other pupil demonstrates another. This difference raises the question of how we should aggregate achievement in geography. How should we describe the overall achievement in geography of these two pupils when compared with a pupil who demonstrated both characteristics of better explanation which we have identified at around level 5?

This question was explored by investigating the responses of 114 pupils to three questions which were designed to test achievement in 'Environmental Geography' (Attainment Target 5) at levels 6 and 7. The questions are reproduced in Figure 13.4. Answers to question 1 could easily be divided into those which referred to one point of view only and those which referred to different points of view (as requested by the question). Answers to 2a could be divided into those who referred to erosion of paths in general terms only and those

1 Look at the Ordnance Survey map. Why might the following disagreement arise: between people living in Blaenau Ffestiniog who want the disused local quarries to be reopened and people who are against the idea?

2 Look at the Ordnance Survey map. Explain how an increase in the number of visitors to the area could threaten:
   a) the quality of footpaths
   b) the character of the area.

3 One problem facing the Snowdonia National Park Authority is overcrowded car parks. A proposal has been made to double the number of car parks and extend existing car parks in squares 6441 and 6541. What additional problems might be created by the proposal?

Figure 13.4: Environmental geography questions in pilot KS3 test, Summer 1993

Qn	Total number of pupils giving a higher level response on this question	Also scored at least one 0	Gave lower level responses on each of the other questions	Gave two higher level responses	Gave three higher level responses
1	16	2	4	5	6
2a	14	4	4	4	2
2b	19	1	2	10	6
3	13	1	3	4	5

Figure 13.5: Environmental geography responses to questions in KS3 pilot tests, Summer 1993

who referred to paths being widened or getting more muddy. Some answers to 2b only referred to a specific change (e.g. in use of buildings), some only referred to a general change in character (e.g. 'becoming busier', 'more touristy'), whilst others provided a specific illustration of a general change. Answers to question 3 either mentioned an immediate effect (e.g. 'cutting down trees to make a car park'), an effect which was not immediate (e.g. 'there'll be more pollution with the cars coming to the car park'), or they provided an example of each. It was very noticeable that those who provided an example of each conveyed a sense of time in the long term effect ('more cars will come making it noisier') in a way which was absent from the answers of those who only referred to a 'non-immediate' effect. On this basis the answers to each question were defined as either 0 : either omitted or no acceptable answer; 1: lower level of acceptable answer — which in questions 2a and b included all answers which referred to a specific or a general change, and in question 3 included all answers which referred to either an immediate or a non-immediate effect; 2: higher level of acceptable response. The answers of all pupils who offered at least one higher level response in the other questions are summarized in Figure 13.5. Although the sample size in Figure 13.5 is small, there are clearly some patterns emerging. Higher level responses to question 2a (on the effect of visitors on footpaths) are unrelated to the level of response on other questions. However, the number of pupils given a higher level response to each of the other questions does appear to correlate with the totals of higher levels of responses to the other questions.

Conclusion

The evidence of this analysis of pupils' test answers suggests that it is possible to identify different qualities of thinking which are specific to geography, but which are transferable across questions and across some events, patterns or circumstances. Some of the observable differences in the pupils' responses are not indicators of a higher level of thinking, whilst others clearly are. The significant differences in quality revealed in this analysis can be grouped under three broad headings of specificity, contextualization and viewpoints and perceptions. From an assessment point of view, the advantage in identifying qualitative differences of this kind is that marking can be linked to an evaluative process of discriminating between qualities of pupils' geographical thinking. This would open a formative concept to testing and marking rather than continuing a reliance on pupils' recalled descriptions and explanations, while avoiding grading answers on the basis of mental processing or language skills which are clearly not specific to geography.

References

CHRISTIE, T., BOYLE, B., DAVIES, P. and SCHIAVONE, T. (1993) *CFAS Evaluation KS3 Geography Pilot Tests*, Centre for Formative Assessment Studies, School of Education, University of Manchester.

DRIVER, R. (1983) *The Pupil as Scientist*, Oxford, Oxford University Press.

LAVE, J. (1992) 'Word problems: A microcosm of theories of learning', in LIGHT, P. and BUTTERWORTH, G. (Eds) *Context and Cognition*, Hemel Hempstead, Harvester Wheatsheaf, pp. 74–92.

List of Contributors

Annabel Charles is Project Officer — University of Cambridge Local Examinations Syndicate.

Peter Davies is Lecturer in the Staffordshire Business School, Staffordshire University. He was principal geography researcher on the CFAS/SEAC Key Stage 1 and Key Stage 3 geography Standard Assessment Task development (1991–93).

David Dean is Research fellow in CFAS School of Education, University of Manchester. He was principal researcher on the 1994 mathematics cross-key stage comparability exercise (SCAA).

Keith Drake is Adviser to the Vice-Chancellor on External Initiatives, University of Manchester.

Professor Wynne Harlen OBE is Director of the Scottish Council for Research in Edinburgh.

Ben Jones is Senior research associate with the Northern Examinations and Assessment Board (NEAB), Manchester.

Professor Roger Murphy is Dean of the Faculty of Education at Nottingham University and President of the British Educational Research Association (BERA). He has written extensively about educational research and assessment.

Peter Ratcliffe is Research Associate with the Northern Examinations Board (NEAB), Manchester.

Colin Robinson is Former Director of the School Examination and Assessment Council's (SEAC) Evaluation and Monitoring Unit (EMU). He is Principal Evaluation Officer at the School Curriculum and Assessment Authority (SCAA).

Professor Terry Russell is Director of the Centre for Research in Primary Science and Technology (CRIPSAT) at the University of Liverpool. CRIPSAT is contracted to SCAA for development of the Key Stage 2 science tasks and tests for England and Wales in 1995–97.

Kari Smith is Senior Lecturer at the Oranim School of Education of the Kibbutz Movement, Haifa University, K. Tivon, Israel.

Dr John Townshend is Educational Consultant at the Organization for Economic Cooperation and Development (OECD).

Ian Walker is Assessment Director for the International Baccalaureate.

Andrew Watts is Project Director — University of Cambridge Local Examination Synicate.

Dylan Wiliam is Senior Lecturer in Education at King's College, University of London.

Index